JUDITH -

THANK YOU FOR YOUR KIND COMMENTS. AS YOU CAN SEE WE THOUGHT THEY WERE MORE THAN A COVER QUOTE + MOVED THEM TO A SPECIAL FOREWORD.

Pau!

The Conflicted Leader and Vantage Leadership

Franklin University Press
2006

Library of Congress Cataloging-in-Publications Data

Gray, Al—Author
Otte, Paul—Author
The Conflicted Leader and Vantage Leadership—1st edt.
Includes index.
Library of Congress Control Number: 2005937932
ISBN: 1-931604-04-5

Printed in the United States of America

Our sincere thanks to the United States Marine Corps for allowing us to reference the book FMFM1: *Warfighting*

Franklin University Press
201 South Grant Avenue
Columbus, Ohio 43215-5399
614-744-8335
leader@franklin.edu
www.leadership.franklin.edu

Contents

Foreword

by Judith M. Bardwick

Starting in the mid-1980s, *leadership* became the vaunted key to solving every economic and social issue. That model of *leader*—Jack Welch and Lee Iacocca, for example, were regarded as models of excellence—were people who seemed able to find the most perfect solution and, in a top-down barrage of effective communication were able to bring the rest of the effected population into line and on board.

With the focus on *leaders,* few people noticed that in a period of escalating change that very little was predictable, that no one person at the top of the heap could possibly have solutions to problems at all levels and parts of an organization, or that a top-down/down-up bureaucratic form of communication was an unforgivable waste of time in a period when time was truly money.

The American military, especially the Marine Corps, rather than Corporate America, has turned the concept of *leadership* on its head. Reviewing the new reality of a greater number of unknowns than "knowns," of instant communication between anyone, anywhere, of warfare waged by loosely confederated groups of enemy instead of organized massed troops, the military decided that *leadership* would depend on the presence of *leaders* throughout their organizations.

At the very time that much of Corporate America was saying that employees were the organization's key resource, employees' input was neither acknowledged nor welcomed in the top-down messiah model of *leadership*. Just when Corporate America largely abandoned its long-term commitment to its employees and demonstrated a lack of conviction in their employees' abilities, the U.S. Military did exactly the reverse.

The military turned the concept of *leadership* on its head when it demonstrated its belief that *leaders* could be found in all ranks and in all specialties when everyone was given training to act as a leader and understand what *leadership* required of them as individuals. The Marines believe the personal qualities it takes to make decisions in an ever-changing environment of conflicting data and changing probabilities require intelligence and boldness, a willingness to act and take the initiative when you're not certain, an internal moral compass and personal ideals and ideas you're willing to go all the way for.

The Marines know their culture must expect and accept reasonable mistakes because a "zero defects" mentality stifles boldness and action, which are *leadership* imperatives. More than any other unit in society, the American military knows that today's *leadership* needs *leaders* who can imagine what is possible even if it is unlikely. Vantage *leaders* can stay focused despite an unrelenting barrage of uncertainty, can remain conceptual and not be blinded by unending computer-generated minutiae, and their commitment will not falter despite a hard road to victory.

We owe General Al Gray USMC (Ret.) and Dr. Paul Otte great thanks for bringing us a very clear and convincing description of the U.S. military's and especially the U.S. Marine Corps extraordinary success in creating leaders and a culture of leadership throughout the organization. The military genuinely believes there is potential in most people. It is that profound belief in the potential of their members that allows them to fully develop all of everyone's potential.

Judith M. Bardwick—author of *Danger in the Comfort Zone* and *In Praise of Good Business*.

Introduction
The Teacher and the Scholar—
The Journey to Vantage Leadership

by Paul Otte

If you only look for leadership in the usual places, you will only find the usual leadership. Think about it. To many, the search for leadership is a process of trying to create certainty in an uncertain world. Too often, people are looking for the secret, a "recipe for success," when the answer may be obvious, although they fail to grasp it. They go beyond simple, only to get lost in the complex. Waiting for someone else's solution, they fail to develop their own.

As a teacher, I have long held the belief that our students (especially older students) learn as much, or more, from each other than from their professor. Likewise, as their professor, I have benefited greatly from the time I spend with our students. In many ways, the faculty to student, teacher to scholar relationship embodies that of the leader to follower. Our students bring their experiences into the classroom, challenging us, as well as helping us understand and strengthen our beliefs about leadership.

This is especially true in our undergraduate Leadership Philosophy class, where we develop our students' abilities to find leadership in places they wouldn't normally look. They begin by identifying a leadership philosophy (which we define as a system of ideas and ideals) in a children's book of their choice. It is easier than it may seem at first suggestion. After all, children's books are full of examples of individual character and values, common elements of leadership. They also document leadership in movies and books not considered to be about leadership. It's fascinating to see how students develop their natural curiosities and open themselves up to new ideas.

Their most difficult assignment (from the students' perspective) is to write a paper about leadership by observing an activity (not in their work environment). Most seem to procrastinate, looking for the perfect activity. As a result, they frequently end up using an event that occurs close to when their papers are due. Examples have included watching children and animals engaged in play, family and community functions (including funerals), events in nature, and emergency situations. One student wrote about people on an elevator and concluded with the insight that too many people want to reach the top (be leaders) by pushing the (elevator) button, versus taking the stairs (doing what's necessary).

Another student observed her niece as she led her Barbie dolls. The 3-year-old set the goal, directed the dolls, promised rewards at the end, and even told them the potential consequences of any inappropriate behaviors. This prompted considerable class discussion about how others (those we call society) can (and unfortunately, most likely will) destroy the natural leadership demonstrated by this 3-year-old. To me, the discussion reinforced my belief that when in doubt about leadership, ask (or observe) a child. I owe this insight to my own daughter, Deanna Kropf, who is the director of a large child care center and has been a major contributor to my leadership understanding and development.

What else can we learn from the students and their assignments? Like our students, you may have struggled with the difference between management and leadership. I remember a time when I looked at management theories as a continuum that ultimately led to leadership. Beginning with the scientific approach of Fredrick Taylor, moving to the behavioral theories and the debate about whether the emphasis should be on tasks or/and people, and ending with the theories often called situational, or contingency, it is easy to conclude that leadership is simply an extension of the people side of management.

But I have learned leadership is much, much more. This has been reinforced time after time as our students report on the leadership they observed in their selected activity. Leadership is a phenomenon separate from, as well as significantly different than management. Management activities emphasize process, power, and control. Leadership activities are based on relationships between the leader and the follower in the accomplishment of a positive goal. In discussions with students about their chosen activities, the dissimilarities become very obvious. Although they initially struggle with the difference between management and leadership, their observations help them as they develop the intuitive ability to recognize the distinction. If you are still in doubt, consider observing an activity and drawing your own conclusions.

What else have I learned from these student activities, as well as my own experiences? That leadership is a natural state. At first this statement may seem to confirm the belief that leaders are born, not made, but that is not the intent. In my opinion, this ongoing debate can best be answered by saying that all leaders are born, but their "birth as leaders" may not correspond to their natural birth date. Instead, I believe there are triggering events that give birth to leaders and leadership. Before all this sounds too academic, we should return to the statement that leadership is a natural state.

To understand this better, let's go back to our discussion about management and leadership. To many, management is the "normal" state and leadership the exception. But I believe the opposite. We are "born" as leaders, but others (society, in general) often draw leadership out of us as we are converted into a management way of thinking. I remember reading Betty Edwards' book *Drawing on the Right Side of the Brain.* It is her belief that our ability to draw is directly tied to our age when we stopped drawing. How many of us have taken drawings from our children or grandchildren and proudly displayed them in our offices and on our refrigerators? Were these works of art? Yes, in their natural (undeveloped) state. But then what happens? We teach our children that trees are green (not purple) and to stay within the lines by introducing coloring books. They stop developing their artistic talent and we turn budding artists into those who simply color.

Betty Edwards suggested that when pictures are turned upside down people could create better drawings because they wouldn't be limited by their past experiences. Again, if in doubt try it. But more importantly, let's apply her concepts to leadership. If leadership is a natural state as proposed, we should be able to observe it, in an unadulterated state, in our children. Remember the student's activity of observing her niece leading her Barbie dolls? What will happen to turn this natural leader into a manager? What are the management equivalents of the "trees are green" and "stay within the lines?" In a natural state, children test their assumptions. Tell a child to not touch the stove because it's hot and then watch as they do. Sooner or later, we break them of this behavior, only to tell them later, as adults in leadership development programs, to "break all the rules" and "think outside the box."

Ask a child a question and you will get an honest answer. When children follow their natural curiosity and ask why, they may be told "because I am the parent." No wonder later in life they accept (or give) answers like, "that's they way we have always done it," or "it's not in the budget." We applaud the individuality of children, but too often look for conformity in the work environment. We are told that the brain wave activity of a preschool child is many times that of an adult. Is it a wonder that after introducing excessive structure into their lives through the educational process we are then told the creativity level of a 40-year-old is only a small fraction of that of a 5-year-old?

Like the artists who never stop drawing, the best leaders may be the ones who keep developing their leadership talent, taking it to higher levels. They continue to test their assumptions (asking why and why not), give honest answers (to help themselves and others), stay creative despite the processes working against them, and along the way develop their natural curiosity and, with it, their leadership.

Are there other situations where leadership can be observed in a natural state? From my experiences, the military in general, and military conflict in particular, offer clear examples in support of my premise. If you have never served in the military, you have not had the opportunity to observe it first hand and will need additional examples. If you have served, you already know there is a special bond between leaders and followers. But unless you are currently on active, reserve, or national guard duty, you may not be aware of the complexity of leadership in the military today.

Before we explore this in depth through our discussion of Vantage Leadership, there are some common themes we can take from our discussion of leadership as a natural state. Both child and military leadership are based on uncertainty and conflict. Children turn to each other to be led through the new, the uncertainty of growing up in today's world. In the military, warriors follow the leader on night patrol who they believe will "accomplish the mission and return them safely." In business, people follow leaders who they feel will take their organizations beyond survival to thrive in today's environment.

In discussions with my faculty colleagues, we have come to the conclusion that uncertainty, chaos, and conflict are the prime reasons for leadership. If there is certainty and no one is resisting your efforts, management may be all that is needed. Rules, procedures, and process work in a certain world. You are expected to "stay within the lines." If there ever was a point in our history when management alone was adequate, today's ever-changing world has shifted the emphasis to leadership. But as stated above, leadership is not simply an extension of management. It is based on a relationship between the follower and the leader in the accomplishment of a (positive) goal. If the followers believe they can accomplish their goals by themselves, they might also feel leadership is not needed. But before you misinterpret this statement, realize that in a world of perceived certainty (what we would call complacency), a leader will create a vision that is uncertain (goals that go beyond the expected).

How many times have we heard that a leader needs a vision? To us, a leader needs uncertainty and conflict (the prime conditions) for leadership. A vision statement is not an end in itself, but only a means to demonstrate a need for leadership. Is leadership needed? It depends on how you view the state of change. If you read the first four chapters about the waves of change and can still believe that we live in a certain world, nothing may convince you that there is a need for leadership in any form. But, if you conclude that today's leader is in conflict because of these waves of change, then you, like many of us, may have been searching for a new form of leadership.

Let's discuss the sources of, and the relationship between, uncertainty and conflict. This may seem like the "chicken and the egg question." You may see the impact of change, but question if you are really in a state of conflict. Or you may feel in conflict, but are uncertain about its causes. In some ways it is like the concept of stress. The source itself (of uncertainty, as well as stress) may not be as important as our reactions to it. Uncertainty is often the "price we pay" for change. Conflict is both born in uncertainty and creates uncertainty.

Conflict is created by the reaction of others (as well as oneself) to uncertainty. Yet the most destructive conflict (in the military, business, and life) can come from trying to create certainty in a world of uncertainty. Like stress, uncertainty can come from external sources or be self-induced. A vision can, as noted above, be a source of self-induced uncertainty, a reaction to externally created uncertainty, or (as is often the case) a combination of both forces.

Observing this interplay between uncertainty, conflict, and vision has helped us see that leadership exists at various levels (not necessarily related to the hierarchical level of a leader). The key is to find, nurture, and turn loose those who demonstrate the potential for a higher level of leadership. How can we identify these leaders? At higher levels of leadership the vision of a leader is more possible than probable. In other words, their vision stresses what can be, rather than simply extending what is. It is the leadership equivalent of "coloring outside the lines." At higher levels of leadership, leaders are opportunistic. They create change, resulting in greater uncertainty.

Keeping focused on the accomplishment of the possible despite increased levels of uncertainty requires a higher level of leadership. Attempts to create certainty can greatly reduce a leader's ability to stay focused. Pursuing the possible (opportunities) while maintaining momentum (staying focused) despite uncertainty and under conflict is an ability we have observed in leaders who function at the highest levels of leadership.

Remaining conceptual, being able to see the forest and not just the trees, in the face of increased conflict and uncertainty caused by external as well as internal factors (like impending timelines) is further evidence of a higher level leadership. To us, conceptual is a way of thinking based on a leader's philosophy. A leadership (not an academic) philosophy is defined as a system of ideas and a sum of ideals (personal convictions). A leadership philosophy is best conveyed through intent and example. Simply put, it is "doing the right thing, in the right way, for the right reasons."[1]

Higher levels of leadership require higher levels of commitment. Again, like our definitions of conceptual and philosophical, our meaning of commitment goes beyond the norm. It includes a devotion to the people a leader is given responsibility for, a sense of duty to the people and the organization, and a dedication to the possible (the vision). A commitment is more than being committed. Consider leaders who accept a position but "keep their bags packed," waiting for the next step in their career (a promotion, or a new position). They can be very committed, but it is to their own career, not the people and the organizations they serve.

At higher levels of leadership, leaders become subordinate to the people, placing their needs ahead of their own. Does this mean those functioning at the higher levels of leadership are not promoted, or selected for other (higher level) positions? Not hardly. These leaders are the most sought after, but are often too busy pursuing the possible, staying focused, and doing the right things to actively pursue other positions on their own.

We have all observed leaders who operate at these higher levels. They are the ones we are most likely to follow. We may disagree on how many there are, or even the success of specific leaders, but one thing is certain—we need more leaders with the abilities to see opportunities, maintain momentum despite uncertainty, and remain conceptual in conflict. How can we identify, develop, challenge, and promote those with the abilities to take leadership to its highest levels? This is the critical question in a world that is becoming more uncertain every day, the world that has created the Conflicted Leader. Where can we find the answers?

There is a new model for leadership, one that transcends the waves of change and the revolutions. It has led to success through every revolution: social, behavioral, and military. It is a higher level of leadership that brings together the concepts, ideas, ideals, and values we will discuss through the context of the revolutions. We are calling it Vantage Leadership because vantage is, by definition, superiority in conflict.

Vantage Leadership is built on a very special foundation; the philosophy of the 29th Commandant of the U.S. Marine Corps, General Al Gray, as documented in *Warfighting*. Surprised? You might be even more surprised to learn how different people took completely different paths to the same conclusion. One, Christopher Washington, Chief Academic Officer of Franklin University, received a copy of *Warfighting* from one of his MBA students. The second, me (Paul Otte), has spent the last ten years on a journey of understanding and applying *Warfighting* under the guidance of General Gray. Imagine my surprise when Christopher Washington said to me, "This is a great book on leadership that should become the foundation for our MBA program." That comment and my (not surprising) positive response gave birth to a new Franklin University MBA curriculum, the Vantage MBA, and the request from a third person, Pam Shay, Franklin University's MBA Program Chair, to write this book.

In Dr. Shay's words—

> "Vantage leadership is best defined within the context of ever-evolving waves of change. From the agricultural change wave to the emerging judgment change wave impacting our lives today, leadership remains a central driver toward success. As chaos, uncertainty, and conflict—hallmarks of the judgment change wave—become increasingly viewed as natural states that can create great opportunities, the reality is that neither individuals nor organizations move from one change wave to another at the same rate or in uniformity. Therefore, Vantage Leadership embraces the reality of the conflicted leader—one who must lead individuals and organizations co-existing in multiple change waves through the opposing 'clash of ideas and values' that define each wave."

"As a Marine would say, 'aye, aye,' Christopher and Pam," but first let me tell you about my journey and introduce my teacher, General Gray.

> "The relationship between an officer and enlisted men should in no sense be that of superior and inferior, nor that of master and servant, but rather that of teacher and scholar. In fact it should partake of the nature of the relation between father and son."
>
> General John A. Lejeune, USMC, 13th Commandant, 1921

My journey began in 1995 when a series of fortunate events led to my first meeting General Gray that summer. Immediately, I sensed the personification of General Lejeune's wisdom, quoted above. I was a former enlisted Marine (who left the Corps in 1965 as a Corporal after serving for four years) and he was an officer. He had been the highest-ranking officer, the Commandant (1987–1991), and he is called by many the modern-day Chesty Puller (the most-respected Marine warrior ever). I quickly felt the teacher and scholar relationship, but this time I was the scholar and General Gray the teacher. I suddenly felt that I might be at the beginning of the greatest learning experience of my life. Looking back, that now seems like an enormous understatement.

General Gray told me that learning about *Warfighting* and the philosophy imbedded in it was the beginning of a journey. He further advised me that, "it will take you where it takes you." Where has it taken me? To a realization that General Gray's philosophy is the answer to developing leaders who can operate at the higher levels of leadership, under uncertainty and conflict.

Marines may represent the largest "brotherhood" in the world. It became obvious that my journey was advanced because I was part of this common bond. This was especially evident in my more than three dozen interviews, across the nation, with former Marines in key leadership positions in business, government, and education who not only took the time to meet with me, but also openly discussed with me their experiences and values. More importantly, they shared their beliefs that the philosophy set forth in *Warfighting* not only contributed to their leadership success in the Corps, but is equally applicable to leadership at the highest levels in any setting.

General Gray is a great leader who consistently operates at the highest levels of leadership. As I write this, I can picture the look on his face as he reads it. And I can visualize his other looks. From the twinkle in his eye and the smile across his face when he sees a fellow Marine and how the smile widens even further if it is an enlisted Marine (General Gray began his career as an enlisted Marine, rising to the rank of Sergeant before receiving an officer commission during the Korean War), to the emotion in his eyes when he thinks about "his Marines," especially those who were lost serving our country.

Few people take the time, or have the opportunity, to set forth their personal beliefs. Fewer still live their lives, in everything they do, based on their philosophy. And only a handful impact the lives of so many through their leadership as demonstrated in their words, deeds, and actions. General Gray is one of the special few, but as he would remind me, it isn't about him. It is, as the Foreword to *Warfighting* states, about his "philosophy on warfighting. It is the Marine Corps' doctrine . . . it provides broad guidance in the form of concepts and values. It requires judgment in application. The thoughts . . . represent not just guidance for actions . . . but a way of thinking in general."[2]

In this book, my teacher has joined with me (the teacher, turned scholar) to respond to Christopher Washington and Pam Shay's request to create a new "foundation for our MBA program." Together, we will provide them and you the broad guidance, a new way of thinking, found in a new model for leadership. Not one from the usual places, but one based on the philosophy found in *Warfighting*. We will explain and demonstrate through examples how this new model for leadership can develop leaders who can operate at the highest levels, under uncertainty and conflict.

Remember also Pam Shay's comment, "Vantage leadership is best defined within the context of ever evolving waves of change?" Before we can discuss a new model for leadership, we will discuss how (as Pam says), "Vantage Leadership embraces the reality of the conflicted leader—one who must lead individuals and organizations co-existing in multiple change waves through the opposing 'clash of ideas and values' that define each wave." I agree, Pam, and along the way we will merge this clash of ideas and values with the concepts from *Warfighting*.

What about you and your search for leadership? If you are a Vantage MBA student, a Marine, or a leader in a business, community, education, military, or government organization, we are confident you can develop the judgment needed to apply our guidance, philosophy, and way of thinking at the highest levels of leadership in any setting. My journey took more than ten years. Are you willing to invest the few hours it will take to read this book?

> "Throughout history, the way men and women make war has reflected the way they work."
>
> Alvin and Heidi Toffler, 1993[3]

THE CONFLICTED LEADER AND VANTAGE LEADERSHIP

By General Al Gray, USMC (Ret.) & Dr. Paul Otte

FRANKLIN UNIVERSITY PRESS
2005

Prologue

Imagine yourself leading during the American Revolution. Clearly it was an exciting time. It was a period of great uncertainty for America and its leaders, then and future.

Now imagine yourself leading during four revolutions, all impacting you in the same time period. How many would respond, "That's what it means to be leading today?" We doubt anyone would. Yet, today's leaders are expected to handle great change and uncertainty brought about from four revolutions.

What revolutions, you might be asking? The answer is the revolutions that are part of the "waves of change." Sociologists have identified the first three waves of change and their corresponding revolutions. The first wave, the Agricultural Revolution, began thousands of years ago. The second wave, Industrial Revolution, started only hundreds of years ago. The third wave, Knowledge Revolution, began impacting us sometime in the middle of the 20th century.

And now, ready or not, there is another wave. The fourth is already underway and we are calling it the Judgment Revolution. These waves of change have been greatly compressed over time. Some of today's leaders began their careers during the Industrial Revolution and have witnessed first hand the coming of two more revolutions, Knowledge and now Judgment.

Even today's newest leaders find themselves working with people and in organizations that seemingly can, and do, bear the characteristics of the Industrial, Knowledge, and Judgment Revolutions simultaneously. And if you look beyond America's borders, there are countries that are still in their Agricultural Revolution. If you thought it would have been exciting to lead during only one, the American Revolution, imagine how much more exciting and challenging it is to lead during four revolutions.

Hopefully, this brief introduction begins to explain the Conflicted Leader. The dictionary defines conflicted as "a clash of ideas." That seems to be an accurate description for leading under the influence of multiple revolutions.

To help in your understanding of, as well as acceptance of, the Conflicted Leader, we will begin by looking at leadership through the revolutions (Chapters 1 to 3). By examining a series of factors: values, technology, and knowledge, supported by time, size, and certainty (and its opposite uncertainty), along with responsibility, relationships, and role, we intend to make a strong case for a new leadership model.

We will introduce and discuss (in Chapter 4) the fourth wave; the one we call the Judgment Revolution. We will explain how we have identified the next revolution and how this great change is already impacting us. The first three waves of change were outlined by shifts in employment, but this fourth wave has been driven by behavioral factors and defined by success.

Then we will describe (in Chapter 5) a new archetype for leadership that has been shown to be amazingly resilient through every revolution, sociological as well as military. Where have we found our model? In an institution that is older than America itself—the United States Marine Corps. Is it hard for you to believe such flexibility in an organization that you might view as highly structured, and relying on intense discipline?

Discipline, thought by many to be an automatic action applied without thinking, is different today. To the Marines, a well-disciplined unit, or person, is one that does what must be done. The Marine Corps' best weapon is the individual Marine and, in turn, the individual Marine's best weapon is his or her mind. Rote is still used as a technique to get the recruit through boot camp, but its purpose is to identify potential. Are you surprised? For now, we hope you are at least intrigued.

We call our new form of leadership Vantage. One dictionary defines vantage as "a position giving a strategic advantage, commanding perspective, or comprehensive view."[4] Another definition, "superiority in conflict,"[5] seems even more relevant to our discussion about Vantage Leadership and the Conflicted Leader.

We will present Vantage Leadership through the higher level of leadership themes of seeing the possible over the probable, staying focused despite uncertainty (without creating certainty), remaining conceptual in conflict, having commitment, and a sense of presence. Our discussion will introduce a new (maneuver) way of thinking (as developed by the Marines), built on the concepts of concentration, speed, surprise, boldness, friction, uncertainty, fluidity, disorder, philosophy of command, commander's intent, decision making, focus of effort, shaping the situation, and mission tactics.

We will provide you with examples of how the themes and concepts can be part of any organization. We will challenge your way of thinking and encourage you to apply the concepts in your own world of chaos, change, and uncertainty. Unfortunately, if you are looking for "leadership secrets" or a "checklist for success" you will not find it here (or anywhere else). What you will find is a way of thinking in the form of guidance. It requires judgment, your judgment, in its application.

All of this may seem inadequate for a conflicted leader wanting control over, elimination of, or even victory over, the conflict he or she is experiencing, but conflict is the pervasive and continuing result of today's multi-revolutionary times. The vantage we are "defining" will enable you to lead during these conflicted times, not by controlling or defeating the conflict, but by understanding, applying and experiencing a new form of leadership—a leadership that recognizes uncertainty, disorder, risk, and the waves of change as natural states that create great opportunities for achieving and sustaining the vantage perspective (described in detail in Chapters 6 to 10).

We have defined Conflicted and Vantage, but what about Leader and Leadership? Have you ever thought about how many books on leadership never define the word leadership? Have you ever questioned why we have the word pairs: lead and follow; leader and follower; leading and following; but only leadership, not followership? Most likely you haven't; but we have been wondering on your behalf, and here's what we have come to realize.

People confuse the words leader and leadership and use them almost interchangeably (often in the same sentence). Both are important terms and both (per the dictionary) are nouns, but in our way of thinking the differences are significant. While there may be no commonly agreed upon definition of leadership (each author and each leader may have their own), there are common elements—a leader, a follower, and a goal. While leader is more descriptive of a position, an opportunity to lead, leader<u>ship</u> depicts a relation<u>ship</u>, between a leader, those he or she is privileged to lead, and an end state, the achievement of a goal.

It is the end state that separates leadership from those "leaders" who can only tell us what's wrong with a situation, but lack a goal. These people are often quick to tell us the problems with our leaders and will even state their desire and willingness to lead, but until they add a goal (a direction), how can we (or anyone) follow them?

This is even more meaningful in our definition of leadership because, for us, the goal must be positive for leadership to occur. Based on our definition, leadership is the relationship between a leader and a follower in the achievement of a positive goal; there can be no negative leadership. Some debate this, pointing to leaders who have moved people in negative directions. We agree there are negative leaders, but there should never be negative leadership.

This may seem like a small point to many, but we will quickly counter by pointing out that the absence of something is not best described by inserting negative in front of it, but by creating a whole new word. After all, we don't call it negative swimming. We call it drowning. But this (maybe small) point aside, if we define leadership as the relationship between a follower and a leader in accomplishing a (positive) goal, then we can understand why there is no need for the term followership.

Had enough definitions? Before beginning Chapter 1, there are two disclaimers worth noting. First, as part of discussing plagiarism recently, we learned a new word (source—Robert Harris[6]). The word is cryptomnesia, and it's defined (not in a dictionary, but on the Internet) as hidden memory. It can explain how people think an idea is original when it is actually based on something they have seen, written, or experienced and forgotten.

What's the point? It's our way of saying that we will always do our best to identify the original sources of the ideas that end up in this book, but may not always remember how and where an idea or concept originated. To the many people who have in some way contributed to what is in our minds as well as in this book, you have our thanks and, as often as possible, our acknowledgement.

Our second disclaimer of sorts is our preference for simplistic versus complex explanations. There are many who can provide (and have provided) greater depth to the concepts and ideas that will be discussed. Like many people, our attention span drops off when complicated explanations are given. In reverse, retention is greatly increased when you can think of ideas and concepts in plain, even visual, terms. Simplistic, to us, does not always mean brief. We are both prone to story telling, analogies, and examples to reinforce our ideas. Our goal is to present the ideas and concepts underlying the Conflicted Leader and Vantage Leadership in a simple, straightforward, and focused manner. Before this starts sounding too academic and makes you wonder if it's worth continuing, let's get started.

CHAPTER ONE

The Conflicted Leader— The Waves of Change and the Agricultural Revolution

Like many others, we were first introduced to the waves of change through the work of the great social thinkers and futurists Alvin and Heidi Toffler. *Future Shock*, published in 1970, set the foundation for the tremendous changes that were already underway. In their 1980 book, *The Third Wave*, they focused our attention on the three revolutions: agricultural, industrial, and knowledge. Their concepts were further reinforced in 1995 with a masterpiece of only 128 pages, *Creating a New Civilization*, which brought together their previous writings in a fresh new way with the addition of new chapters to their lives' work.

What follows is not a review of their work, nor a series of quotes from their books. That is neither our purpose, nor our presumption. Their work has shaped the thinking of many people and has provided a foundation on which we all can view the future (as well as the present). What is presented here is based on our interpretations (and perhaps in some ways, misinterpretations) of what they have taught us. It is written without specific references back to the works of the Tofflers. If you would like to form your own perceptions, we would highly encourage you to read any or all of their writings.

There are many sources of conflict for today's leader, and the waves of change are only one source, but they are a significant one. These changes, and the revolutions that accompany them, provide the context in which most other changes can, and (in our opinion) should, be viewed. They provide us the "prism" by which we can understand, apply, and evaluate leadership through the revolutions.

Why use a prism as a symbol for our discussion instead of a lens? The word choice is worth discussing. Over the years we have grown to realize that the waves of change cannot be viewed as linear revolutions when applied to leaders and leadership. This may appear contradictory to the societal definition of the revolutions. To many, the revolutions are triggered by a shift in the work force, output, or resources of a country or region, or from one type of employment to another (i.e. agricultural to industrial, or industrial to knowledge). When a new sector becomes dominant, a revolution is underway. From a leadership perspective, this linear focus can lead to conflict.

By its very nature a society is prone to make assumptions about all its members. Properly applied, a society reflects the will of the majority. But we lead individuals. Even though a majority may share a common view, leadership is based on the relationship between the leader and the follower. And the follower (or the leader) may hold beliefs contrary to the majority. We also know that every individual is unique and can respond to the same action in a way different from others. These differences are major sources of conflict for today's leader. The Conflicted Leader must function in all the revolutions, with all people he/she is responsible for, all at the same time.

Does this mean the Tofflers' work doesn't apply to the Conflicted Leader? No, not at all. As stated above, it provides the context for our discussion, our prism. What leadership concepts can best be viewed through the revolutions? What concepts have been common to leadership over the waves of change? What generic ideas can help us understand a leader's conflict brought about by each of the four revolutions? Could these ideas become "characters" in our leadership story?

The main concepts in our story are values, technology, and knowledge. Values, on the individual level, include principles and ultimately, a person's character. In an organization, values are reflected in a culture. A simple definition of technology is applied science. Over time, science has been applied in various ways from creating weapons for the nomadic hunters, to the earliest machines, through the introduction of computer technology, and to today's world of electronic wizardry. Knowledge is gained from education and experience. Education does not always result from formal classroom instruction. It can be learned on the job and is often transferred, in formal and informal ways, from generation to generation.

All three of our main characters have played an important role in each of the revolutions and in leadership. Like leadership, these concepts have been transformed over time. There have been interesting interplays between them throughout the waves of change. Viewed in their totality, they are defined by the revolutions.

Like any good story, our main ideas have been aided greatly by several supporting concepts. The key ones are time, size, and certainty. Time is more than a point in history. During periods of change, time becomes more meaningful as an indicator of speed, the pace of change. Sustained speed is momentum, a key concept in our new model for leadership. Like time, size has many facets. It is more than being larger. It is a concept that can create a way of thinking, such as mass production or mass advertising. There is a distinctive relationship between speed and mass that we will discuss as attrition and maneuver when we turn to the Marine Corps as a basis for our new model, Vantage Leadership.

Certainty, and its related ideas of structure, rules, and procedures, as well as its opposite, uncertainty, are integral to our understanding and application of values, technology, and knowledge. Some say people seek certainty, while others see opportunity in uncertainty. Viewed as a continuum, certainty and uncertainty become underlying factors in leadership during each of the revolutions and can highlight the difference between management (we manage certainty) and leadership (we lead through uncertainty).

Just as values, technology, and knowledge are the main concepts in defining the revolutions, our leadership "heroes" are responsibility, relationships, and role (what a leader does). Like the other ideas already introduced, responsibility also includes the related concepts of authority, power (and empowering), and delegation (including intent). Relationships are the key to our understanding of leadership. By our definition, the most significant relationship is between the leader and follower, but there are other relationships that leaders must consider in applying these concepts. They include the individual and the institution, colleagues, peers, and other influencers.

Role is based on what is expected from a leader by the followers, as well as the leader's own expectations. In reviewing leadership through the revolutions, we can see how the various roles a leader plays (such as communicator, decision maker, and visionary) have, or have not, been altered in response to the waves of change.

In addition to the leadership factors of responsibility, relationships, and role, we will also view leadership through the functions of management. Some may find this odd, thinking that management is in some way competing with leadership. Not surprising, since many have written about the differences between management and leadership with a stated preference for leaders over managers. There are others who view leadership as an extension of the people side of management. As you will see when we build on these concepts in future chapters, we see leadership as much, much more. The differences are very real, in our opinion, because the roles differ.

A simplistic difference in the roles was proposed by Grace Hooper, the first female Admiral in the U.S. Navy: "Management is for things and leadership is for people." Similarly, Jim Kunk, President of Huntington Bank, Central Region, told a Franklin University leadership class "you manage process and lead people." As proposed above, we manage certainty and lead through uncertainty (a concept we will probe in greater length in our discussion of the fourth wave, Judgment Revolution). Given these role descriptors, you can see how the same individual will frequently function in the role of both leader and manager. Exploring these role differences throughout the revolutions will allow us to better understand leadership.

Some might still question using the revolutions as the context for our conflicted leader discussions. After all, doesn't leadership take place in an organizational setting? Sure it does, and therein lay additional sources of conflict. To assure proper application of our concepts, we also briefly include in our discussions, when applicable, the organizational disciplines of accounting and finance, marketing, human resources, and strategy. In addition to this discipline-based focus of a business, we (you) should consider the life cycle of an organization applied over the revolutions.

At this point, you might be wondering if we have too many concepts to be considered in detail as we move through the waves of change. Remember our preference for simplistic versus complex explanations. You might also remember (from the Prologue) our belief that retention is greatly increased when you can think of ideas and concepts visually. The chart on page 26 summarizes the above discussion.

The concepts (in italics) will not be discussed in great depth. Nor will they be applied to every setting. We will leave that up to you as you apply them in your own organization. The goal is to present the concepts in plain terms, supported by stories, analogies, and examples to reinforce the ideas. It's time to get started.

To truly understand the drastic changes that have occurred over time, picture yourself as a hunter or gatherer in the nomadic age. Without a permanent "home" you are faced with the daily search for food. If you are a man, you would be expected to be a hunter. Women, you would be the gatherers, whose daily search for grains and fruits would become critical if the hunters failed in their role. Not being historians, and certainly not ones who have any special knowledge of this period, we can only hypothesize on our leadership factors during this pre-agrarian period.

Nomadic values may have centered on the survival of the fittest. Education, how to hunt or gather, would have been passed from one generation to another. Technology was limited to the weapons used for hunting. Time would be the immediate, the need for food coupled with defending against aggressors. Size would be limited by the need for mobility and the availability of food. Hunting, it would seem, would be subject to great uncertainty and risk, minimized by the success of the gatherers.

Leadership, if we can call it that, would be expected to be acceded to the best and presumably the strongest hunter. The leader would have the authority and power, subject to continued successes. Not knowing, one might assume the leader felt a sense of responsibility to others for keeping them well fed and safe (although the lack of refrigeration may also have been a motive for the distribution of food to others). Relationships were most likely at a very basic level, and with mobility, might have lacked a sense of permanency. The

Vantage Leadership		
Chapter	Waves of Change	Underlying Concepts (Applied to all waves)
1	Agricultural Revolution	*values* - principles, culture *technology* - applied, science knowledge - education, experience
2	Industrial Revolution	*time* - speed, momentum *size* - mass *uncertainty* - certainty (management)
3	Knowledge Revolution	responsibility - authority, power *relationship* - leader, follower *role* - communicator, decision maker
4	Judgment Revolution	

leader's role would focus on making the decisions of where and what to hunt. The primary role of managers may have been the upkeep of the (temporary) gathering spot.

This is an overly simplistic view to be sure, but if you have transported yourself back in time, it serves our purpose. If you are thinking as a hunter or gatherer, then you can imagine the tremendous and fundamental change that would occur with the coming of the Agricultural Revolution.

Assume for a minute you were a futurist and you could see the "handwriting on the wall" (and of course, there would be handwriting on the wall). You might see that as weapons improve, along with techniques for processing and storing food (canning, drying, and curing), there would be a change underway, one that would lead to people (tribes) settling in one place. Instead of being hunted, animals could be contained until needed for food. In addition, instead of gathering fruits and plants, seeds could be planted and crops would be harvested.

In an agrarian civilization, people now have a home. The early farms were generally small, family affairs. As a result, values were tied to the family. They were strong values, uniting the family and the local community. In many cases, these values would be based on religious beliefs. Initial technology would be limited to farming tools. Science (basic by today's standards) would be applied to farming and the improvement of the crops. Like the nomadic period, education would be transferred from family to family, generation to generation.

Ultimately, we saw the beginning of the local schoolhouse, but education took a backseat to work on the farm. Children performed their morning chores before school and returned in time for afternoon and evening responsibilities. The school year began after the crops were harvested in the fall and ended in time for spring planting. It's hard to ignore that our school year today is still rooted in the agrarian calendar (while the structure, rules, and procedures seem more fitted to the industrial period).

During the Agricultural Revolution time was an interesting concept. Coupled with the uncertainty brought by environmental factors, such as weather, the farmer would have to take a longer view. The farmer also saw a need for long periods of sustained pace when crops were planted and harvested. Although there were day-to-day risks associated with finding food in the nomadic period, the risks intensified in the agricultural period when entire farms were lost due to crop failures. Still, compared to today, the farmer took a much longer view.

The size of the farm was frequently limited by the number of workers available and this was generally tied to the size of the family. When available (and affordable), helpers were seen as hired hands. Their role was limited to backbreaking manual work. The father was generally the leader of the farm business, while the mother led the family. (At times, the mother's leadership would be direct and acknowledged, while in other situations it would be more indirect.)

Obviously, the agrarian mother played a key human resources role by "producing" the workers. The leader and the followers were family first, and the workers (children) respected and obeyed their parents. Authority and power rested in the parents who clearly saw themselves as responsible for their children. Relationships between the leader and the followers, the foundation in our definition of leadership, were frequently an extension of the relationship between parent and child. Even with the addition of hired hands, the leader and follower relationship was still focused on family. Often these workers brought their families with them, working together as well as living on the farm.

It seems doubtful that the farmer saw his role as a business leader. It would be even less likely if the mother saw herself in any leadership role. In reality, it seems safe to assume that both demonstrated leadership in many ways, direct and indirect. Community leadership was supportive as people welcomed new families to the area, helped each other in times of need, and banded together against common enemies (including the weather). Government leadership, especially at the local level, came through town hall meetings. Educational leaders, often the teacher in a one-room school house, were respected (although, as noted above, education was a lesser priority than farming).

The land owner took the risks and earned the profits, if there were any. The farm is an asset that can, and ultimately must, be transferred to another (generally the next) generation, creating a life cycle for the business. In comparison to today, it must have been a hard life, and it is difficult to imagine anyone feeling entitled. Hard work was a main focus as the efforts were directed toward the land and the crops. Leaders, at every level, would have led by example. The end state (what everyone was working toward) may have been simply survival.

Perhaps our view of the leader in the first wave, Agricultural Revolution, has been formed through watching too much TV in our earlier years. Our descriptions may be a combination of *The Waltons*, *Bonanza*, and even *Gunsmoke*. But we believe most people have similar perceptions of the leader in the first wave—a pioneer, who faced great adversity and uncertainty, relied on family values, demonstrated strong character, and accepted hard work. There was limited help from science and technology. The greatest technological advances would have occurred near the end of the period with the introduction of farm machinery.

Our view is also centered on the American farmer and the fact that we are a relatively young country. In older societies, the role of the farmer differed greatly by nation and region. In other countries, those in power were often royalty, in positions of kings and lords. The relationship between the leader (king) and followers (farmers) was one of servant to master. In America, where farmers came to escape the ruling royalty, decision making became more participatory.

Yet today we look back to these older societies in an attempt to understand the beginnings of leadership. From the western world, we read about philosophers like Plato and Aristotle. Some have studied Machiavelli's advice to *The Prince* for guidance on how to rule. Military rulers, like Alexander the Great, have also become popular. From the eastern world, Sun-tzu's *Art of War* is considered by many as an example of strategy and leadership applicable to modern times.

As noted above, the Agricultural Revolution's impact on society lasted over thousands of years, spread over many generations. While this lessened the impact on any one individual, the cumulative impact over time was substantial. The most significant visible change over these thousands of years may have been in technology.

At the beginning, the tools of the farmer would have been minimal. Looking back, the plow was a major innovation, first pulled by the ox, then the horse, and finally the tractor.

In the latter part of each wave, new ways to increase productivity are developed. With fewer people needed to create the same level of output, changes in the demand for products or services result and a shift in employment occurs. Increasing technological innovation was a major factor in the wave of change from agricultural to industrial. As more and more technology was invented to aid the farmer, the emphasis shifted from the land to the machine.

When did the second wave, Industrial Revolution, begin? That depends on where a person lived and who is telling the story. Certainly it is a relatively recent phenomenon, with its beginning between 200 and 300 years ago. Of course, some societies and countries today are still tied to the land. In leading industrial societies, like England, the Industrial Revolution is generally felt to have begun in the middle of the eighteenth century, sparked by technological advances, such as James Watt's improved steam engine (1763) and the philosophies of Adam Smith, as set forth in the *Wealth of Nations* (1776).

The United States was not far behind. The shift from agricultural to industrial was felt during both our war for independence, the American Revolution (1775–1783), and our Civil War, where the industrial North was in conflict with the agricultural South. While it would be overly simplistic to say the situation we face in today's world, with the clash of values and ideals, is a continuation of the conflict between agricultural and industrial societies, it surely is a contributing factor.

As we said in the Prologue, leading during the American Revolution would have been exciting. But the Conflicted Leader must cope with the impact of multiple revolutions, all having an impact at the same time. The next step is to understand and learn how to apply the lessons learned from the second wave, Industrial Revolution.

Vantage Leadership

Chapter	Waves of Change	Underlying Concepts (Applied to all waves)
1	Agricultural Revolution	*values* - principles, culture *technology* - applied, science *knowledge* - education, experience
2	Industrial Revolution	*time* - speed, momentum *size* - mass *uncertainty* - certainty (management)
3	Knowledge Revolution	*responsibility* - authority, power *relationship* - leader, follower *role* - communicator, decision maker
4	Judgment Revolution	

CHAPTER TWO

The Conflicted Leader—The Second Wave, Industrial Revolution

It is doubtful that many in the early days of farming thought of themselves as leaders or managers. It was the Industrial Revolution that introduced us to most, if not all, of the management concepts we discuss today. Although the second (industrial) wave lasted more than two hundred years, many of the changes had a major impact on people's lives from the very beginning.

Industrial workers often were required to move from the farm to urban areas, bringing their families with them. Not only did work change, but living conditions and relationships were also drastically altered. Working away from the home, the industrial worker, initially the father, had less time to be with other family members.

Looking back, it was common in both the agricultural and industrial periods for workers to be called "hired hands." (Ostensibly, they were not hired for their minds.) Farming required working with hands, as did manufacturing. But in an industrial setting, there is another change. The emphasis shifts to the machine, and the workers, unless skilled, are considered interchangeable. Machines are the assets. Along with the focus on equipment and the large investment it required came shift work, standardization, specialization, structure, control, and the superior/subordinate, management/worker relationship. Profits and power belonged to the owner of the factory.

Thinking by workers was generally neither required nor encouraged. More and better machinery led to mass production, economies of scale, and larger and larger (more powerful) businesses. Did everyone accept these changes? No, there were early resisters. The most well-known were the Luddites in Britain. Reacting to the changes that threatened their jobs, they smashed the machinery.

The introduction of the assembly line further reinforced the secondary nature of the worker and added to people's resistance to the demands placed upon them. Along with the increased emphasis on reducing work to its smallest element, the assembly line and its repetitive tasks also created additional pressures on worker satisfaction and retention. Although not often discussed, the assembly line created massive labor problems at Ford Motor Company, where turnover reached "380 percent for the year 1913 alone. So great was labor's distaste for the new machine system that towards the close of 1913 every time the company wanted to add 100 men to its factory floor, it was necessary to hire 963."[7] Ford's answer—"$5 a day." High wages bought worker recruitment and retention, although most likely not satisfaction or motivation.

Consistent with the changes underway, early management theories emphasized a scientific approach. Time and motion studies were used to determine the most efficient (although not necessarily the most satisfying) way to produce a product. Each step toward efficiency reduced the workers' need and opportunity to think for themselves or the company. Organizational structures stressed control. Often based on early military models, these structures were also very hierarchical, utilizing multiple layers of supervision. As a result, the concepts of span of control; line and staff; and centralized, top-down decision making were developed and emphasized.

As a reaction to the increased structure, labor unions came into existence to represent the workers and collectively offset the power of management and owners. To assure fair treatment of workers, unions emphasized working conditions, job skills, and consistency of actions and reactions. As more and more "improvements" were negotiated for the collective worker, the individual continued to lose any incentive for taking initiative, exceeding expectations, or even thinking. Responsibility and accountability were determined (and allocated) by contract. Often wages, salaries, and performance increases were negotiated by position or grouping, not by individual abilities or performance.

Later management theorists shifted from a scientific, productivity orientation to a behavioral approach. The watershed study occurred at the Hawthorne, Illinois, Western Electric Company plant in 1924. Researchers, led by Elton Mayo, selected a small group of workers and then increased the lighting levels to determine the effect on productivity. The result was higher productivity, but when lighting levels were decreased, worker productivity went up again. The (then) surprising conclusion—paying attention to people can increase their performance. This widely known study is often credited as beginning the human relations (behavioral) approach to managing people.

Early factories employed "fitters" whose job it was to make sure that parts moving through the production process fit together. As industrial businesses grew, middle managers became responsible for a new type of "fit." Their positions became critical in reducing the time necessary for information to flow from the top to the bottom (and data to flow from the bottom up) in an often complex organizational structure. Management became a profession, and middle managers, the new "fitters," kept the day-to-day operations moving while providing a bridge (often over a chasm) between the top management (generally the owner) and the workers.

Positions directly related to producing the product were designated line, and the organization's "line" stretched from the worker "on the line" to the CEO. At the lowest supervisory level, the "foreman" was the management (line) control point to assure that the worker produced a quality product (what), at an assigned position (where), met schedules (when), and followed procedures (why). In general, workers did not think about how the process or the product could be improved. Thinking was reserved for those managers further up the "line."

Middle managers also provided an informational and control link between line and the growing staff positions, which were added to improve efficiencies, control assets and expenditures, monitor short-term results, increase certainty, reduce risk, think and plan (strategically) for others, and convince every possible purchaser of a need for the highest margin products (selling, and later marketing). The resulting bureaucracy led to specializations and detailed job descriptions, from the laborers to a wide array of vice presidents. Titles, the business equivalent of military rank, became critical in establishing responsibility and accountability. Corporate headquarters expanded, and power rested in the hands (and minds) of a select few. At the top, the Chief Executive Officer (CEO) was expected to provide the vision for organizations that were becoming more and more myopic.

During the industrial period, the educational system was expanded to include training directly related to developing skills needed for work. Employers expected the schools to provide workers with the basic skills, knowledge, values, and attitudes needed to perform in a business setting. Vocational or trade schools were used to prepare students for the skilled trades. Apprentice programs often bridged the gap between formal education and on-the-job training. Higher education, initially available primarily to the rich or gifted, was viewed as a requirement for management or professional level positions. If already employed, a college degree was seen as a vehicle for promotion. (Despite all of these changes, it is interesting to note that the agrarian-based school calendar persevered.)

Some may view this description of the Industrial Revolution as too simplistic. Others may think it too harsh. It is not our intent to treat lightly or judge negatively the major accomplishments our country made during the second wave. The Industrial Revolution, although generally considered as having begun in Britain, may have been perfected in the United States. We became the world's leading producer in many categories. Our industrial might contributed greatly to our country's military victories during both World Wars I and II. Our major companies were and are respected as world leaders. Any negative connotations are more from our looking forward than from any attempt to suggest that much of what we developed was not needed. What we are today we owe in great part to the contributions of our industrial workers and management.

Nor is it our desire to present a comprehensive history of this period or a management primer. The background concepts we have presented can easily be discussed and reviewed from many different perspectives and in considerably more depth. Instead, it is our goal to identify the major sources of conflict that were born during the Industrial Revolution that, along with other third and fourth wave factors, have created today's Conflicted Leader.

As noted above, it is hard to argue against the positive legacy created by the Industrial Revolution. Nor can we ignore the impact this period has had on the worker (follower) and management (today's leaders). The conflict that seemed apparent from the very beginning seems to have continued throughout the period, intensifying with the introduction of unions. As we will see in our discussion of the third wave, the emphasis on the machine (technology) ultimately led us to the Knowledge Revolution. But, in our opinion, the conflict continues today as many businesses and managers are still functioning in accord with the key concepts, beliefs, actions, and results of the second wave, Industrial Revolution. As we move forward in our discussions, we will continue to consider these ideas and ideals, along with the search for certainty through structure and control, including the impact on relationships, and technology, brought about by machinery.

Looking back, it would seem that the clash over values was destined from the very beginning. With the strong emphasis on family values developed over centuries during the Agricultural Revolution, the shift to the company values of the Industrial Revolution must have been very difficult to accept at the individual (family unit) level. Not only were families forced to move, but often they found themselves in "company towns," where company values could impact them not only at work, but also through the influence the company would have on the stores, the schools, and even places of worship. In the song *Sixteen Tons*, Tennessee Ernie Ford tells of "owing his soul to the company store." The values clash occurred in many ways; the most noticeable conflicts were (and are) found in the concepts of power, size, structure, and the search for certainty.

If we had to select one concept that best characterizes this conflict and guides many of the resulting beliefs and actions, it is power (control over others). As businesses grew rapidly during the last one hundred years, power intensified while at the same time becoming increasingly centralized (more power in the "hands" of fewer people). Along with increases in the size of businesses, there came more complexity reflected in increased structure. This was evidenced by more and more layers of management, centralized decision making, and bureaucracy. Power (like size) in itself need not always be negative. It is the result of power, along with individual perceptions of and reaction to the powerful, that have the greatest impact on people. The more people feel removed and isolated from those who control and assign their tasks, resources, and rewards (i.e., information, budgets, and merit), the more they see power and size as dangerous to their destiny.

A significant outcome of the emphasis on power and size (in the industrial period) was a mass approach to business. With a focus on mass production, what others and, in particular, the customers, wanted was often not considered. Remember the statement attributed to Henry Ford, "They can have any color car they want, as long as it's black." Mass production, not surprisingly, led to mass advertising with an emphasis on reaching the greatest number of people at the lowest per unit cost. Management used the power of mass advertising to sell people the products with the greatest profit margins.

An additional negative result of both power and size for the institution as well as the individual is an inflated reaction time. Decisions requiring approval by multiple layers of management often lack timeliness. Information flowing vertically through increased levels of supervision can be delayed and distorted. Fortunately for big businesses during the industrial period, if a new company tried to enter the marketplace by emphasizing speed and responsiveness, it could be "defeated" by high entrance costs (machinery), restricted access to resources (raw materials), temporarily reduced prices, and, of course, increased mass advertising by the large and powerful.

The concept of power and its emphasis on increased size, coupled with a mass approach to producing economies of scale, created an emphasis on efficiency. All this led to the goal of controlled and ultimately reduced costs. Lowering expenditures requires and emphasizes an understanding of fixed and variable costs and cost accounting. For maximum efficiency, everything must be reduced to the smallest unit. The production operation is studied, and each task is analyzed in minute detail. There is a scientific approach to production (i.e., parts control and just-in-time inventory) and to people's work (time and motion studies).

Results are measured in quantitative terms: cost-per-unit, profit margin, production/sales per employee, and earnings per share. Exceptions (variances from established standards) in financial and other quantitative reports are highlighted and analyzed. The emphasis is on identifying and correcting problems. With repetitive tasks, there is little freedom for the individual to improvise. Making production routine is seen as a way to assure that profits are proportionate to sales. With a focus on short-term results, uncertainty is often ignored.

To improve efficiencies and benefit from economies of scale (through increased size), rules, procedures, and processes provide needed control through enlarged structure. Rules are seen as defining acceptable actions and behaviors. Managers, especially those in the middle "ranks," are relied upon to monitor processes and assure adherence to rules. As procedures replace individual thinking, people frequently hear the response, "That's the way we have always done it." Using the financial process for control purposes leads to comments such as, "It's not in the budget." Some managers use structure as a barrier to avoid developing relationships with (getting to know personally) the people they supervise (another form of control).

No wonder many have come to view control as an obstacle to and a disincentive for taking individual initiative. Even if rules are intended only to set guidelines for behavior, some may see them as limiting what can be done, i.e., if the rules and procedures do not specifically authorize an action, do not do it. This perception is reinforced if creativity is seen as desirable by management (for example, new product design, research and development, creative departments in advertising firms, or reengineering teams), but a special environment is provided, frequently in a different area or location, so as to not "contaminate" the established controlling structure.

The primary industrial assets are physical: factories and machinery. Mass production is based on the premise that plant capacity (a quantitative measure) and worker output should be maximized. The process is relatively simple. Machinery turns raw materials into finished goods. People, especially in the lowest, non-skilled positions, are viewed mainly as the operators of the equipment. Equipment is costly, and to maximize the investment in machinery, people (the operators) are often required to man the equipment in multiple shifts, around the clock, seven days a week.

To ensure efficiencies, required skills are documented, often in great detail, in job descriptions. Each worker is responsible for a small part of the process and held accountable for predetermined quantitative results. The emphasis is on the skills needed to keep the machinery running. Training and rewards are based on production needs and results. An underlying assumption is that workers need little information beyond that required to perform their specific tasks, as long as they follow established (control) procedures.

Consider the common practice of tagging (for inventory purposes) all machinery and equipment. The message sent is that the organization cannot afford to lose valuable physical assets. Although no person would want to be "tagged," many might like to feel they are at least equally valuable. One only needs to look at a company's financial statements for further (negative) reinforcement. Physical assets are recorded and valued. Yet there is no dollar value assigned to people, even though many businesses now say people are their most important assets.

It is easy to make comparisons between these second wave themes and the actions of businesses during the industrial period. Power is paramount. There is strength in size. Economies of scale resulted in the creation of huge corporations. And the larger the business unit, the greater the need (at least perceived) for a methodical and scientific approach to how goods were produced and decisions made. Much time was spent on passing information up a "chain of command" and waiting for a decision to be sent down. The emphasis was on centralized control. With more controls over the processes, along with increased (at least until recently) levels of management and supervision, movement (most often seen as decision making) tended to be ponderous and tempo and momentum difficult to develop and sustain.

The industrial model uses structure to provide control. Innovation and initiative are not encouraged. Industrial results are viewed in quantitative terms and in a shortened time frame (quarterly financial statements). There is a strong belief in results proportionate to efforts, with greater expenditures (generally capital resources) expected to create greater results (reduced costs). Machinery and equipment are the primary resources. People are important for the skills they bring to operate the equipment. Because the emphasis is on relative strength and the efficient application of massed resources, control is generally centralized. Second wave companies often create large corporate staffs. The search for certainty leads to centralized control and an inward focus on corporate procedures and the "corporate way."

Think of an organization familiar to you that may still operate under these beliefs. It might attempt to be an industry leader by using mass advertising to maintain a dominant market share, using supreme resources to keep all competitors in a weakened position. Focusing on efficiencies, it might lower costs in any way possible. Because results would be judged in quantitative terms, people (a non-quantifiable variable) could and would be replaced by technology (machinery) whenever possible. There might be acquisitions of suppliers to add to the superiority of the business. Management's focus would be on a scientific approach to handling its employees.

Entire industries might be characterized as relying on these second wave ideas and ideals. Consider the automobile industry. Prior to being forced to change by foreign competition, these attitudes seemed prevalent. Models with the highest profit margins could be sold by the mass "power" of advertising. The automobile industry is not the only evidence of such thinking. Today, we are focusing our attention on education; it has become a national concern. But haven't educators followed practices associated with second wave beliefs? We have created larger and larger school districts that have become slow to react to changes in society. We have been led to believe that our problems would be solved by adding more resources. The more we spend, the greater should be our results.

On a national level, there has been an emphasis on the large industrial firms—"The Fortune 500." Our country is seen and often judged on the basis of the actions and results of the biggest companies. Success for the second wave company is based solely on numerical results. Often, results are not based on competency, but on sheer numbers of people, facilities, and equipment. Does this mean that business managers who followed the second wave industrial thinking were wrong? No! Looking back, this approach has generally been successful. Our country has enjoyed great superiority in technology and in numbers. Likewise, in the industrial period our businesses were superior world leaders. Looking forward, however, an entirely new approach is needed.

Before we can present, understand, appreciate, and apply a new leadership, we must look to the changes brought about by the third and fourth waves of change. The Knowledge and the Judgment Revolutions have shifted our way of thinking, but the conflict continues.

Vantage Leadership		
Chapter	Waves of Change	Underlying Concepts (Applied to all waves)
1	Agricultural Revolution	*values* - principles, culture *technology* - applied, science *knowledge* - education, experience
2	Industrial Revolution	*time* - speed, momentum *size* - mass *uncertainty* - certainty (management)
3	Knowledge Revolution	*responsibility* - authority, power *relationship* - leader, follower *role* - communicator, decision maker
4	Judgment Revolution	

CHAPTER THREE

The Conflicted Leader—The Third Wave, Knowledge Revolution

There is little doubt that the Industrial Revolution had, and continues to have, a major impact on our society. Even though the industrial sector no longer employs the majority of Americans, manufacturing firms remain critical to our nation's success. The values, concepts, and practices of the industrial era are still guiding the overall philosophy of some organizations. And within most, if not all, organizations there are individuals who are still following industrial management concepts.

Looking back we saw how changes in machinery (technology) were a major underlying factor in the second wave change from the Agricultural to the Industrial Revolution. You might have already concluded that technology (now driven by the computer) created the third wave of change. Many observers of societal change would agree with you. While we would generally agree, our ongoing interest in education and leadership leads us to propose an additional driving force. As noted above, our industrial might contributed greatly to our country's military victories during World War II. But after the war came the GI Bill, and veterans returned home and went to college in record numbers.

College, no longer available only to the rich and gifted, now became an earned right of those who served our country. In our opinion, this created a major force for change: the higher education of the general population. Even without technological change, wouldn't the industrial superior/subordinate model have been challenged by a (higher) educated workforce? We think so. In addition to the mass increase in veterans attending college full-time while living on campus, the GI Bill also changed higher education by increasing the numbers of working adults attending college at night. Both of the changes—college access and adult education—have given our country a global competitive (knowledge) advantage.

While the second wave is synonymous with the Industrial Revolution, there is not the same general agreement as to the revolution created by the third wave of change. It has been called the Information Revolution, the Technology Revolution, and, by some, the Postindustrial Revolution. Others refer to the Knowledge Worker as the product of the third wave. It is not our intent to select one word at the expense of the others. A strong case can be made for any one of these titles to describe the third wave, but this is where our preference for simplistic over the complex comes in to play. To us, the term Knowledge Revolution encompasses the pervasive changes in technology, information, and education that together create knowledge.

It is worth noting, however, the reference to the third wave as postindustrial. The Industrial Revolution made such an impact on the world as we know it today that in many ways it continues to set the framework for our discussion. As already noted, those who study change say a new wave occurs with a shift in employment. Clearly, the Knowledge Revolution came from such a shift. The majority of people no longer directly produced a product (postindustrial). Most were employed in technology, information, education, or other service sectors. And many in industrial firms, as well as farmers who can fertilize their crops based on Global Positioning Systems, do knowledge work.

The reference to the postindustrial age seems especially true in regard to our discussion of managers and leaders. In our review of the second wave, Industrial Revolution, we reported the most noticeable conflicts were found in power, size, structure (controls), and the search for certainty. Not surprisingly, many of the new ideas created in the third wave are defined in anti-industrial terms. Empowerment, rightsizing, and reengineering are prime examples.

Empowerment changes the superior/subordinate relationship in the Knowledge Revolution. Individuals are given greater authority to make decisions. Levels of management are reduced. Working in teams, people are encouraged to build on differences. Recognizing the power of the customer, marketing efforts are altered. Technology allows businesses to "customize" their products. Downsizing (for efficiency) is replaced by rightsizing (the implication being that the right size can be larger or smaller). Processes are reviewed and reengineered to remove years of bureaucracy (unnecessary controls). Structure is reduced as companies move toward a more relaxed "business casual" work environment. Technology (the computer) drastically changed how and where people work and how information is processed. With information being more widely dispersed, second wave "Controllers" (in the true meaning of the title), who see their role as cost accountants and the "keepers of the budget," are replaced by financial services-oriented team players who implement activity-based costing and revenue enhancement programs.

With workers empowered and information readily available, middle managers were eliminated in large numbers in most organizations in the Knowledge Revolution. This is an interesting phenomenon. Many have viewed the reduction in layers of management as being driven primarily by a need for reducing costs (efficiency). Others saw middle managers as part of the bureaucracy (control) and as "casualties" in the move to empower people. After all, the middle managers fought for years to gain a modicum of power from top management only to see large shifts in power move past them to lower-level workers. It would only be natural for middle managers to resist such changes, consciously or subconsciously.

These views may be at least partially accountable for the demise of middle managers, but they may have been doomed even if efficiencies and empowerment were not emphasized because their roles, like the "fitters" of the past, are no longer needed. Many middle management line positions were created during the Industrial Revolution to reduce the time required to process information and to think for the workers at lower levels (or to keep them from thinking). With technology, information flows with little or no time lag between those who have it and those who need it. As a result, the information "float" was reduced to zero, and middle managers became expendable.

While the concepts of empowerment, rightsizing, and reengineering moved us forward and resulted in a change in emphasis from managers (second wave) to leaders (third wave), they are, as noted above, more anti-industrial reactions than entirely new approaches. They do represent improvements, but consider the ways they have been presented. Most often they are discussed and applied in the terms and themes from the second wave, Industrial Revolution. For example, empowerment still treats power as a "zero-sum." Giving power to another is not seen as a multiplier.

Transferring power from the top implies that it is "owned" by a superior and that power given to a subordinate could be taken back. In this view, empowerment is based primarily on positional or legitimate power. But there are other sources of power: expert, informational, and reward (to name a few). In the third wave, many of these sources of power shifted from the owner/managers to the individual. Information frequently is possessed by people at all levels, and they have the "power" to share or not to share it with others. Expert power also rests with a broad-based group. For example, how many executives have the same level of computer knowledge as newer, younger employees?

From the behavioral approach, we have learned that the "power" of rewarding people is dependent on the individual. In a diverse society, what motivates or rewards one person can be completely different for someone else. Empowerment motivates some people, while others perceive the increased responsibility as asking them to do more without correspondingly increased compensation. And once power is transferred, can it be reversed without substantially demotivating people? We think not. Empowerment, in its true meaning, is turning people on and then letting them go (and grow).

Rightsizing, as it has been applied, almost always reduces the size of a business. As a result, most people think it's just a different term for creating efficiency by reducing costs. In many cases, rightsizing provides the company an increased chance for surviving in a competitive environment. But we "rightsize" people, and those who remain often feel that the same amount of work (or more) must now be accomplished by fewer people. In addition, they mourn the loss of fellow workers (teammates), and despite assurances, their level of fear increases and their loyalty decreases.

Reengineering, like Total Quality Management (TQM), focuses on processes and procedures with a goal of reducing or eliminating unnecessary controls (products of the Industrial Revolution). TQM seeks continuous improvement, while reengineering begins by asking if the process can be reinvented or eliminated. Both TQM and reengineering, like empowerment, tend to be based on a top-down approach. Teams are created (generally with the "blessings" of top management) to change processes, procedures, and controls, but the teams frequently must present their recommendations to top management for approval.

The key questions are: how did the systems create the bureaucracy that comes with a reliance on controls; and, once improved, will the efforts need to be repeated? When a process is reengineered, do the individuals directly involved take the initiative to prevent bureaucracy from creeping back into the process? Our bias is toward Total Quality Leadership (TQL), a process that would encourage ongoing improvements, initiated at all levels. However, as long as the focus of TQL, TQM, and reengineering is on process, procedures, and control, instead of individual initiative, they are still rooted in the industrial era.

What about technology? What role does it play in the Knowledge Revolution? While technology provided a bridge between the second wave, industrial period and the future, how it is used determines if it is consistent with the second (industrial) or third (knowledge) wave approach. If the emphasis is on the equipment (the physical assets), technology makes people more efficient, it is a second wave concept. But technology can also be applied to support the person. Leaders of the Knowledge Revolution emphasize that their goal is to use technology to "equip the man," a third wave approach, not to "man the equipment," clearly a second wave intent.[9]

Technology is also a mixed blessing. It improves efficiency, but it also places a greater reliance on skills. The individual's level of information can be substantially increased by technology. Although this can lead to new knowledge and provide opportunities for individual development, increased compensation, and self-esteem, an overemphasis on skills can lead to recruiting, retaining, and rewarding people who may have incompatible values, attitudes, and behaviors with fellow workers and the organization. And in a litigious society, since skills are more easily quantified, qualitative (value based) employment decisions may be more difficult to defend if the legal system is still rooted in the second wave, industrial period.

> "Displaced industrial workers thus cannot simply move into knowledge work or services the way displaced farmers and domestic workers moved into industrial work. At the very least they have to change their basic attitudes, values, and beliefs."
>
> Peter F. Drucker[8]

In the Knowledge Revolution, results are no longer solely quantitative. People are recognized as more and more important to the success of a business. People movements, especially in high tech firms, can almost instantly change a company's value. Accountants, long the recorders of corporate history, are still looking for ways to reflect people as assets on a firm's balance sheet. Superiority in physical assets (based on numbers) is becoming a weakness in many industries. Businesses recognize the importance of time (speed) to their busy customers. Shop-at-home services (catalogue, cable TV, and even Internet sales) continue to increase at accelerating rates. The emphasis is on the customer. Mass advertising (the "power" of large corporations) is shifted to one-to-one, relationship-oriented marketing approaches. All businesses talk in terms of "niche," often exploiting others' weaknesses.

> "The marriage of Glaxo Wellcome and SmithKline Beecham will create the world's second-largest company. But size is no guarantee of success."
>
> The Economist (1998)[9]

As we have hypothesized from the beginning, the movement between the waves of change has not been a smooth flow of ideas and concepts, thus the Conflicted Leader. Many businesses (as well as individual leaders) operate under both second and third wave thinking simultaneously. Companies have used innovative approaches to develop new products, drastically cutting the time from idea to market. Many large organizations create smaller business units that emphasize an entrepreneurial spirit. Leaders in small and large businesses talk of the new values. Flexibility, commitment, willingness to take risks, accepting responsibility, and taking initiative are among those most often mentioned. (But workers often note that hiring and promotion decisions are often still based on second wave skills and quantitative results.)

Businesses and individuals are conflicted by the simultaneous application of second and third wave thinking in many ways. Consider how one issue from the industrial era, the allocation of profits, is compounded in the Knowledge Revolution. In an industrial setting, physical assets are depleted during the production process (accountants call it depreciation). Information and knowledge, the assets of the third wave, are different; they expand when used. In addition, more than one person or institution can use the same information, often in different ways, to make a profit. It is difficult to control information. It can be mobile. It is often shared, it "leaks," and it requires a knowledge(able) worker, not a machine, to be useful.

> "Thus knowledge used properly becomes the ultimate substitute for other inputs. Conventional economists and accountants still have trouble with this idea, because it is hard to quantify, but knowledge is now the most versatile and the most important of all the factors of production, whether it can be measured or not."
>
> Alvin and Heidi Toffler (1993)[10]

How then should profits be allocated? In industrial thinking, the owners of the assets, along with those who provide the capital (and assume the risk), share in the profits (although an increasing number of companies have created profit sharing plans for employees). In the third wave, the higher the level of knowledge required, often the less physical assets are needed. Do people own their ideas? What if they were generated during work hours? What about an idea originated away from the workplace that is tremendously relevant to a company's future profits? What about brainstorming sessions where many people share, to some extent, in the thinking process and the results? How should the traditional owners of physical assets and capital and the knowledge workers who create and apply information share in the profits? The answer remains a continuing challenge to the Conflicted Leader.

Near the end of the Industrial Revolution, another shift began that has had a significant impact on the relationship between management and the worker. In the agricultural period, and throughout most of the industrial era, those who managed a business were most often also the owners of the resources. There was little question who would be in charge. It was the owner, the CEO, who generally made the day-to-day decisions impacting the business and the workers. As businesses increased in size, the owner/CEO had to seek outside funding to pay for increased resources, mainly machinery and factories. More and more corporations became publicly held (outside ownership). Initially, CEO/owners were able to maintain a large share of the outstanding stock. But as corporations grew, demanding more and more resources, outside investors and debt holders (i.e., banks) began to play a more important role.

The CEO was no longer in total control and began to answer to owners, a separate group who purchased their stock not to run the company but in search of a reasonable return on their investment. Some stockholders sought short-term rewards, and the stock markets created to facilitate such investments placed great emphasis on quarterly changes in profits. Lenders, although generally not direct owners, exerted considerable influence and expected frequent financial reports on assets (inventories and receivables) and liquidity (cash and cash equivalents).

Owner/CEO financial rewards were often based on a combination of their performance as managers and the return on their investment. When they were sole owners, it was difficult, but generally unnecessary, to distinguish between the roles. When the CEO was no longer the only owner, but controlled through personal and/or family holdings the majority of the stock, the situation became considerably more complex. In theory, the compensation received as CEO should solely reflect performance and results. In practice it is often difficult to determine. When the CEO is a professional manager, selected by the owners' representatives, the Board, there may be more scrutiny.

Much has been written about the appropriate multiplier in compensation between the lowest worker and the CEO, and it is not our intent to add fuel to what seems to be a simmering fire. Our interest is on the relationship between the leader and the worker that results from the shift in CEO ownership and compensation. When CEOs were also the owners, compensation was generally not disclosed or questioned. As companies became publicly held, executive compensation, stock options, "perks," and other benefits, were required to be reported. If non-executives perceive the amounts as not equitable, it can create great conflict and damage. When the disparity is seen as excessive, people may not accept responsibility for communicating problems, opportunities, or suggestions to those who "receive the large salaries."

All of this may have contributed to the theme often heard in the Knowledge Revolution—"What's in it for me?" On one extreme, the most positive reaction would be that people see the answer in maximizing their contributions with an expectation of correspondingly increased rewards. Others may react negatively and feel it makes more sense to reduce their efforts to correspond with perceived rewards. Behavioral theorists have long argued whether money motivates. The answer may be that money can demotivate if it damages relationships, respect, and trust.

Another issue is how to define the real "assets" of a business. Industrial organizations have elaborate controls over the acquisition, disposal, and security of their physical assets. Since these are tangible assets, they can be inventoried and insured. What about the "assets" of information, knowledge, and people? People are mobile. They can leave with their knowledge (although businesses are trying to prevent them from leaving with proprietary information). The value of today's business is often based on the people, the knowledge workers, and the leaders. Even though the intangibles of people and accumulated knowledge are not reflected in a company's financial statements, you could make a good argument that they are reflected in stock prices and market value.

Have you noticed the use of both *are* and *were* in the above discussion? While it may seem grammatically incorrect, it is consistent with our belief that the waves of change, the revolutions, and the resulting concepts, ideas, values, and beliefs most critical to leadership remain with us and are compounded over time. To the sociologist, the revolutions occur when there are major shifts in employment, from agricultural, to industrial, to knowledge workers. To the leader (the Conflicted Leader) the concepts, ideas, values, and beliefs of each period (including the agricultural in some countries and areas) create a cumulative impact on the relationship between the leader and the follower in the achievement of a (positive) goal (our definition of leadership).

The use of both *were* and *are* is also consistent with our conviction that a new revolution is already underway—a fourth wave of change that began in the last few years of the Knowledge Revolution—a change that will have a significant impact on the Conflicted Leader, not by replacing the concepts, ideas, values, and beliefs we have already discussed, but by once again having an effect on the concepts of values, technology, and knowledge, along with the ideas of time/speed, size, certainty, structure, responsibility, role, and relationships.

Are you ready for the next wave of change? Or are you still wondering if the Knowledge Revolution was only a postindustrial shift? After all, most of our discussion of this period presented the changes by comparing them to industrial concepts. We believe there was a significant shift, a wave of change, that created the Knowledge Revolution, but the lasting impact of the industrial era provides a point of departure for what followed. In addition, as we have emphasized several times before, the concepts of the Industrial Revolution provided us the foundation for modern day management.

We moved from the very authoritative (owner) manager in the beginning of the Industrial Revolution to an early scientific, control-oriented approach (both of which gave rise to worker unions), through the introduction of behavioral models and the continuum of management/leadership style, from an emphasis on task to one on people. Finally, near the end of the Industrial Revolution we saw an emphasis on leaders and ultimately on situational leadership which told us the "right style" depended on the situation (which included the follower).

Once we shifted our thinking from machines to people, a new wave closely followed. The Knowledge Revolution moved us from managers to leaders. People, supported by education (formal and informal), new technology (mainly computers), and access to information (created through technology and education) replaced the machine as our focus. The third wave of change also brought greater opportunity, as well as uncertainty.

During the Agricultural Revolution whoever owned the land owned the crops. In the Industrial Model, machines replaced the land as the focus of production, but the concept of the profits (now in the form of finished goods) accruing to the owner continued. In the third wave, where knowledge becomes the focus, the "output" is no longer solely tied to a single owner, as many people can create profits through the same (shared) knowledge. Thus the output of the Knowledge Revolution is opportunity, and along with the opportunity comes greater uncertainty in lost or misapplied opportunities. A knowledge leader warned us years ago that the new companies of the Knowledge Revolution, the "dot.coms, could drown in their sea of opportunities."[11]

As we watched the many Conflicted Leaders who were dealing with the impact of all Revolutions simultaneously, while trying to avoid drowning in their sea of opportunities, we could see a new wave emerging. We saw it in Franklin University students (undergraduate and MBA) and leaders in all settings (business, community, government, and military), as well as the institutions they lead. People in many organizations were moving beyond knowledge, beyond opportunities, to a new focus that applies knowledge, balances it with experiences, and sorts through the opportunities. Not all of us agree on what to call it (some say wisdom), but we have named it the Judgment Revolution.

Vantage Leadership

Chapter	Waves of Change	Underlying Concepts (Applied to all waves)
1	Agricultural Revolution	*values* - principles, culture *technology* - applied, science knowledge - education, experience *time* - speed, momentum *size* - mass *uncertainty* - certainty (management) responsibility - authority, power *relationship* - leader, follower *role* - communicator, decision maker
2	Industrial Revolution	
3	Knowledge Revolution	
4	Judgment Revolution	

CHAPTER FOUR

The Conflicted Leader—The Fourth Wave, Judgment Revolution

How many revolutions can a Conflicted Leader face at one time without drowning? It isn't just a riddle—it describes the real world for today's leader. The answer lies in awareness and leadership. First, the awareness—you might question if there is another wave of change underway. The world around you might look more like the Industrial or the Knowledge Revolution. As we have already seen, it's hard to identify the start, or the end, of a revolution. And because it's difficult, seldom will there be agreement on the number, or descriptions, of the waves of change.

It isn't necessary to reach consensus. What is important is the impact that the changes are having (and will have) on you and your leadership. We could lump them together, give them different titles, change the order of our discussion, or ignore them completely, but they will not go away.

Don't spend your time worrying about the individual waves of change. Instead, focus on the concepts, the ideas, and the ideals, especially as they apply to you, the Conflicted Leader. Leadership follows awareness. Ultimately, we will provide you with a new model for leadership, one that transcends the waves of change and the revolutions. It is a leadership that has been tested in conflict over hundreds of years. We will call it Vantage Leadership, because vantage means superiority over conflict.

Before examining this in more detail, let's make sure we are all following the same definition of judgment. To some, judgment equates to a superior evaluating someone subordinate to them, being judgmental. In the extreme, it can have religious connotations, such as "Judgment Day." Our use of judgment to describe the fourth wave is based on the definitions tied to the ability to make well reasoned choices from existing and possible opportunities. Our exercise of judgment is based on experiences and values. It is an ability shared by many (and able to be developed by many more), not a trait possessed by a relatively few. Remember (from the Introduction) we have replaced superior and inferior, along with master and servant, with teacher and scholar in our way of thinking.

In preparation for our new approach to leadership, our discussion of the fourth wave, what we are calling the Judgment Revolution, will compare, contrast, apply, and (at times) evaluate the concepts and ideas we have presented across all revolutions much in the same way as today's Conflicted Leader is being simultaneously impacted by them. Let's begin. The following visual representation summarizes our discussion through the end of Chapter 3 and introduces the fourth wave, Judgment Revolution.

	Input	**Focus**	**Output**	**Years**
Agricultural (1st)	*seeds*	**land** *Family*	*crops*	*2,000+*
Industrial (2nd)	*raw materials*	**machine** *Managers*	*finished goods*	*200+*
Knowledge (3rd)	*technology information education*	**knowledge** *Leaders*	*opportunity*	*30+*
Judgment (4th)	*knowledge experience opportunity*	**judgment** *Leadership*	*success*	*??*

To some, the shift between the Knowledge and Judgment Revolutions may seem like a subtle difference, or even just a further postindustrial shift. To us, it is much more. In the third wave, the focus changed from the machine to knowledge, creating opportunities. But determining which opportunities to pursue requires judgment.

In the early days of the Knowledge Revolution, the emphasis was on the knowledge worker. We recruited people with the knowledge that could give us opportunities and a competitive advantage. There was a great emphasis on technology workers that was further fueled by computer-to-computer communications, which led to the Internet.

Startup companies were created to capitalize on the changing technology as it was being applied to more and more industries. Tied closely to the Internet, they were referred to as "dot-coms." Frequently valued at great multiples of earnings, or with no earnings, or even short-term prospects for earnings, their value was driven more by hope and the desire to be on the cutting edge than by the more basic financial indicators developed in the industrial era. Lacking a new set of financial indicators, it was difficult to judge which dot-com firms would be successful, or even what determines and defines success. Venture capitalists fueled this dot-com boom by funding many high-tech businesses with the hope that one would become the next Microsoft or Cisco.

Looking back over the revolutions of change, it is our belief that the skills and technology needed in any revolution seem to reach their highest level of development near the end (the last 25 percent) of a wave. And this developmental change then becomes the catalyst for the next wave, the next revolution. It was the improved machinery developed in the final years of the Agricultural Revolution to make farms more productive that led to the second wave, Industrial Revolution. Likewise, it was the technology (primarily the computer) developed to make our industrial firms more efficient that created the shift in focus to technology, information, and education, the precursors of the Knowledge Revolution.

Initially, the third wave of change focused on information and knowledge, its acquisition, expansion, and application. Technology workers in particular could, and often did, freely switch between firms (generally for increased compensation), taking their knowledge with them with the expectation that their skills would add to the new firm's success by creating new opportunities. Many can remember the offices of the early dot-coms. They institutionalized creativity and individual freedom. The knowledge worker created the new firm's culture and challenged older established organizations.

As already noted, the societal waves of change have been tied to changes in employment. It was an easy way to measure the change from agricultural to industrial worker. To see the shift from the industrial to the knowledge worker was a little more difficult. The knowledge worker encompasses people employed in technology, information, education, and the service sectors, but there are industrial (as well as agricultural) organizations that employ large numbers of knowledge workers performing various information and technology functions.

As a result, we believe the concept of waves of change has itself been changing. No longer can we rely solely on societal (changes in employment) factors to identify a new wave. Instead, the pendulum has shifted (starting with the Knowledge Revolution) to a more behavioral approach to recognizing the beginning of a new wave of change. We began to notice the shift from the knowledge to the judgment worker by looking at the dimension of success at both the organizational and individual level.

As discussed above, success in today's world may be difficult to define. The quantitative factors dominant in the industrial era may not always identify or predict success. At the individual level, the change has been even more pronounced. In evaluating the knowledge worker, the emphasis is (by definition) on knowledge. This is most evident in the technology area. What programming languages does the individual know? What technical skills do people bring to their positions? As we move up in an organization, knowledge becomes more difficult to assess. The individuals responsible for evaluating a knowledge worker's performance may themselves have little knowledge or understanding of these skills.

Success then has become more intangible (more behavioral than quantitative), more frequently tied not to skills and knowledge, but to execution and values. In the previous waves of change, judgment was noted primarily by its absence. An individual might have been told he or she had great knowledge, but lacked good judgment. Other early indicators of the lack of judgment include faulty decision making, not "seeing the big picture," poor customer service, missing the implications of one's actions, failure to see (or admit) mistakes, or worse yet—not learning from one's mistakes.

Now, judgment is being included in performance evaluations as an indicator of an individual's success and/or potential. At the organizational level we have seen similar patterns. Much has been written about the poor judgment of some top executives who put their personal gain above the company and the employees. Surely, not all examples of poor organizational judgment reach the level of ethical malfeasance. Most often, the poor judgment is evidenced by decisions with negative results. It could be a new product introduction; a merger gone bad; a promotion or a recruitment that ended with disastrous results; or a series of day-to-day decisions that combined have a significant negative effect on an organization's success.

But don't just take our word for it. Exercise your own judgment. As we compare, contrast, apply, and evaluate the concepts and ideas we have presented across all the waves of change, you decide if and how the Judgment Revolution is impacting you and your organization. Remember, the lines separating one wave of change from another are not always obvious. And even more importantly, remember that the changes are not linear. Judgment has not entirely replaced knowledge. Nor, as we have discussed, has the impact of the industrial, or even the agricultural period been eliminated. As we proposed from the very beginning (and consistent with our title), today's leader is under conflict from all four waves of change, all at the same time.

Just as judgment represents the fourth wave of change, uncertainty is the "tide." It raises (as well as lowers) the level of judgment that is required. Uncertainty is an underlying factor across all waves of change. The major source of uncertainty during the Agricultural Revolution came from the environment. Farmers plant and nurture the seeds, but the crops frequently depend on the uncertainty of the weather. During the Industrial Revolution, structure, controls, rules, and procedures were introduced in an attempt to eliminate (or at least reduce) uncertainty. The Knowledge Revolution, with its emphasis on technology, information, and education created great change which, once again, brought uncertainty to the surface, but seemed to ignore the impact of uncertainty on leadership.

Remember, the exercise of judgment doesn't create certainty, but allows the leader to move forward in spite of the uncertainty. The ineffective leader in the Knowledge Revolution may look more like "the kid in the candy store," seemingly "frozen in place" by the many choices (opportunities) available. The judgment worker recognizes that both danger and opportunity are inherent in uncertainty. But moving forward requires more than a propensity toward action. To be effective, a leader's judgment must be applied within a set of ideals.

Values, principles, and beliefs are the bedrock of judgment at both the individual and organizational level. Agricultural values were family-based, strong on principles, and frequently grounded in religious beliefs. The Industrial Revolution emphasized organizational values, generally expecting individual beliefs to be subordinated to those of the company. And, in the extreme, the company's values focused on production, efficiencies, control, structure, profits, and machines. The pendulum may have swung back to individual values in the Knowledge Revolution, but the "war cry" frequently underlying the knowledge worker's search for values is "what's in it for me?"

As the foundation for judgment, the values in place at a point in time both guide the decisions made and are outwardly reflected in the character of the individual (and the culture of the organization). The farmer's character is one of strong independence, fighting to keep the family together and the farm viable (both as owner and worker). To many, the industrial worker's character was equally strong but frequently under conflict with the owner's values. This conflict gave rise to unions, and the result was a changing perspective. With "collective bargaining" workers lost their individuality. Owners were portrayed as greedy, driven by profitability at all costs. This view changed throughout the Industrial Revolution as workers (and managers) moved from a task-oriented focus to one that was more tolerant (and understanding) of people's values.

The values and character of the knowledge worker have been the source of much discussion and controversy. Some have suggested that the emphasis on knowledge has created a heightened sense of individual importance. Added to this is the ability of the knowledge worker, especially those with higher technical skills, to move freely from one organization to another. But at the same time, organizations have been emphasizing a team approach to work (and play). Not surprisingly, this dichotomy has added to the conflict felt by today's leader.

Like the management theories of the Industrial Revolution attempted to balance the emphasis on task and people, the leadership theories of the Knowledge Revolution have struggled with the conflict between the individual's and the organization's collective knowledge, principles, and values and the ability to apply them successfully in an environment of great change, uncertainty, and opportunity. Principles and values, together with knowledge, create the character of both the individual and the organization—and character builds trust, the prerequisite for leadership.

Our belief, as noted above, is that the change created by the search for the next level of skills (and now values) needed in a revolution becomes both the catalyst for and the identifier of the next wave. If our hypothesis is correct, you can confirm it by looking around. Do you see individuals and organizations that are identifying (and documenting) their values and principles? This goes beyond the written values and goals statements that became popular near the end of the Knowledge Revolution. It is more than printing cards and having them in people's wallets or framed on company walls. It means following, living by, and making judgments based on a set of principles, values, and beliefs. The companies and individuals that are doing this represent the new leaders of the fourth wave, Judgment Revolution.

Another key test of the Judgment Revolution is people's response to the new wave of change. Are people willing to live by a set of values? Do their judgments reflect their ideals? Are people selecting organizations based on a compatibility of values? Do people leave organizations (voluntarily and involuntarily) based on conflicting principles? Do you, or would you? We believe the Judgment

Revolution is well underway. We see it reflected in our own institutions and our people and in other successful organizations and individuals all around us.

It is also evident in the other concepts and ideals we have discussed across all revolutions. Consider speed. Exercising judgment, in spite of uncertainty, increases the speed of execution. A product of the Knowledge Revolution is the abundance of data. While it is generally thought of as good to have more information, too much can slow down decision making. The Paereto Principle, first proposed by Vilfredo Paereto in 1906 and commonly called the 80/20 rule, may be even more relevant today as the Knowledge Revolution has expanded geometrically the volume of information available. The rule proposes that 80 percent of something can be accounted for by 20 percent of something else. Applied to information, it would mean that 80 percent of what you need to know can be found in 20 percent of the data. And in a world of rapid change, knowing 80 percent (with 20 percent uncertain) should allow a leader to (successfully) exercise judgment.

Size is closely related to speed. Early farms were limited by the size of the family. Initially, factories were limited by the availability of machinery, but as the Industrial Revolution progressed mass production became possible. Mass was the keyword during this period. We had mass production, mass advertising, and, in the military, a style of warfare (attrition) that emphasized mass firepower. One only needs to visit the World War II Memorial in Washington D.C. to realize how our industrial might contributed to our successes.

But too much mass (size) can slow down the leader. In the Judgment Revolution, successful leaders are the ones who can create and maintain momentum (sustained speed). Our ability to gain momentum was enhanced by technological advances during the Knowledge Revolution. But too much technology, like too much data, can ultimately slow our judgment as we search for the perfect decision.

The concept of responsibility has also been common to each wave of change. The farmer accepted the responsibility for producing a crop, despite the damages brought on by severe weather. The farmer relied on hard work to overcome adversity. External factors, like the weather, may have been explanations for crop failures, but not excuses. That would be against the character and values of the farmer.

In the industrial period, the owner and the worker became separated and blame became more prevalent. How many times have we heard workers say "it isn't my job, it's not allowed, or that's management's responsibility?" And likewise, how often will managers blame others, the workers, the unions, or the board for their own failures of responsibility? Excuses, excuses, and excuses seem to have been created by, and supported by, the rules, controls, and structures of the Industrial Revolution.

In the Knowledge Revolution, the concept of empowerment was introduced and people were told they had the power and authority to make decisions, but too often the transfer of power was blocked by a worker lacking the appropriate knowledge, or being either unwilling or untrained to accept responsibility. To be successful in any situation requires judgment, and the exercise of judgment is built on the acceptance of responsibility to not only make a decision, but to live with the results (a "no excuses" mentality).

Likewise, relationships have changed over time. In the agricultural period, relationships were found within the family, and even when one went beyond the farm, they found themselves in smaller family type communities. With the Industrial Revolution came larger businesses and expanded cities. Relationships between workers and management were strained, and both tended to build relationships outside of the work environment. Knowledge workers often form relationships with others based on their common expertise or business discipline (technology, accounting/finance, and marketing are examples). To the judgment worker, common values guide decisions, and these values can be shared across disciplines. As a result, in the Judgment Revolution organizations can become "large families" with shared values. Relationships in such a setting become broad and deep.

Relationships impact role. If your definition of leadership is similar to ours (the relationship between a leader and a follower in the achievement of a positive goal) then relationships become even more critical to the leader's role in the Judgment Revolution. In the fourth wave, values not only provide the infrastructure upon which judgments are made, but shared values provide the foundation for leadership. Common values build trust, and trust is a precursor to leadership. The successful fourth wave leader knows that the time to build shared values is before judgment is exercised.

The manager role is dominant in second wave thinking. In the third wave, the emphasis shifts to the leader, but in the fourth wave, with judgment based on relationships, leadership takes the center stage.

With leadership the point of emphasis in the Judgment Revolution, the relationship between the leader and the follower takes on a new meaning. For those who share common values, the role of the leader and the follower becomes more like a colleague and a coach. Like family relationships, both parties to the relationship want the other to succeed, and as a result, both leader and follower more openly discuss strengths and weaknesses. Criticism, when needed, is given to make the other person more successful. Leaders feel an obligation to the people they are responsible for and consider the performance of their people as an outcome of their leadership.

Unfortunately, not everyone shares the same values and principles, even in a successful fourth wave organization. Some may still hold the values (such as structure, control, power, superior/subordinate) common to the Industrial Revolution. Others may have advanced their principles to the Knowledge Revolution and focus on the values related to "what's in it for me?" Differing value sets are a significant source of conflict. The Conflicted Leader learns that this conflict cannot be wished, or willed, away. Like the farmer of the past, today's leaders plant the "seeds of change" through their every action, word, and example. Just as the second wave workers built large industrial plants, today's leaders build relationships from the ground up.

Not surprisingly, education has not kept pace with the waves of change. As discussed previously, most elementary and secondary schools remain on a calendar created for the agricultural era. Their structures, academic and administrative, resemble those of industrial organizations, and what they teach seems (to us) locked somewhere between the second and third (knowledge) waves. Higher education is only slightly more advanced. Technology, although not fully embraced, is more common in college than in high school. Community Colleges, in particular, have been responsive to the needs of employers and have revised their academic programs accordingly. There seems (again to us) to be an inverse relationship between the "prestige" of a university and its responsiveness to the community its serves, including its customers (students).

To the outside observer, our colleges and universities are the harbingers of knowledge, but unfortunately those on the inside know we can be too slow in our response. Some of the best have moved into the Knowledge Revolution and are preparing students for the third wave. Franklin University faculty have gone beyond identifying the fourth wave and have been developing our academic programs, courses, and delivery to meet the leadership needs of today's Judgment Revolution.

But, as already noted, most of the skills needed in any revolution seem to be developed during the last 25 percent of the wave of change. Identifying the beginning of a new wave is difficult enough, but predicting its demise becomes even more difficult. As a result, we do not know if we are in the beginning, middle, or final stages of the fourth wave, Judgment Revolution.

A Second Prologue

We told you in the Prologue that we would challenge your way of thinking. If all of our discussion so far hasn't already done so, perhaps the idea of adding a Second Prologue will, although that's not our sole intent. Typically a prologue precedes the main materials in a book, and that's what we did before Chapter 1. Why then a second prologue? Because it's time to shift our focus, begin our discussion of a new model for leadership, and merge the higher level of leadership themes with the maneuver way of thinking.

Now that we have presented the four waves of change and the resulting revolutions, you hopefully have a greater understanding of, and appreciation for, the conflict facing today's leaders. It's time to answer the question proposed in the Introduction—"Is leadership needed? It depends on how you view the state of change. If you read the first four chapters about the waves of change and can still conclude that we live in a certain world, nothing may convince you that there is a need for leadership in any form. But, if you believe that today's leader is in conflict because of these waves of change, then you, like many others, may have been searching for a new form of leadership."

As promised to you in the Introduction, there is a new model for leadership, one that transcends the waves of change and the revolutions. It has led to success through every revolution: social, behavioral, and military. It is a leadership that brings together the concepts, ideas, ideals, and values we have discussed through the context of the revolutions along with the guidance, philosophy, and way of thinking found in *Warfighting*. It provides the foundation for what we are calling Vantage Leadership. It explains and demonstrates through examples how this new model for leadership develops leaders who can operate at the highest levels, under uncertainty and conflict. We know (hope) you are ready.

For us, the higher levels of leadership themes are a natural progression in a world characterized by chaos, uncertainty, and complexity. They move away from the hierarchal structures of the past, to the decentralized thinking needed in the Judgment Revolution. We have individually, and together, spent a considerable amount of time discussing, debating, refining, clarifying, and confirming the themes. But we haven't changed the conceptual framework.

The idea of a higher level of leadership encompassing the themes of seeing the possible over the probable (being opportunistic), staying focused despite uncertainty (without creating certainty), remaining conceptual (a way of thinking), and having commitment has stood our "test of time," at least in our discussions. We have reinforced our beliefs by presenting our ideas to leaders at all levels, seeking their input. In doing so, we received their overwhelming confirmation.

We have also applied the themes to specific situations demanding leadership. They have proved to be of great help in understanding today's leadership challenges. One example is succession planning. Much has been written about the need to plan for an orderly leadership transition, but many books and articles present the challenge without a conceptual framework for developing and selecting leaders. We believe the higher level of leadership themes are directly applicable to what an organization should be seeking in its current and future leaders.

As noted in the Introduction, the idea of a higher level leadership is presented without consideration of hierarchical levels. Several leaders involved in our discussions suggested the possibility of adding a fifth theme that we felt was more closely related to leaders in higher level positions. We agree with their advice and have added "a sense of presence" which will be discussed in depth in Chapter 10 after we have merged the four higher levels of leadership with the philosophy found in *Warfighting*.

How best to unite the themes with the philosophy became clear as a result of our discussions. While listening to others, we realized the themes of seeing the possible over the probable, staying focused despite uncertainty, remaining conceptual, and having commitment are imbedded throughout *Warfighting*. They were always there waiting for us to merge them with these new themes. Did we need a journey to see them in a new way? Or is it an example of cryptomnesia, defined in the Prologue as hidden memory? Whatever the answer, the result is that this and the remaining chapters are built upon the idea of a higher level of leadership, supported by the concepts and the philosophy found in *Warfighting*.

When first published in 1989, *Warfighting*, often referred to as FMFM 1 by the Marines, became the Marine Corps' doctrine. (See note.) Its intent was to provide guidance for action in the form of concepts and values. It represented a way of thinking that would require judgment in application. It both documented this thought process and demonstrated its successful application. Although written for Marines, the concepts have been applied well beyond the Marine Corps. Today, leaders in every setting are experiencing a new form of conflict created by the waves of change. As a leader, you are being impacted by the new Judgment Revolution, along with the lingering effects of the Knowledge, Industrial, and Agricultural Revolutions.

Note: *Warfighting* was first printed by the Marine Corps in 1989 (often referred to by Marines as FMFM 1). In 1994, a book also titled *Warfighting* was published by Doubleday that included FMFM 1 in its entirety, plus an Editor's Foreword.

Breaking with traditional writing style, our references (the numbers in parentheses after the quotes from *Warfighting*) are the page numbers from the original USMC publication, FMFM 1

If you wish to read *Warfighting*, and we encourage you to do so, you will most likely find the Doubleday version (ISBN 0-385-47834-8) where the page numbers differ slightly from FMFM 1 due to an increased number of pages (110 versus 88).

What follows is a merger of the concepts from *Warfighting* with the reality of today's Conflicted Leader. To preserve the intent, as well as the concepts and values, we will present the concepts in their original wording as often as possible using ellipses (. . .) when we delete passages only relevant to the military and limiting restatements only when necessary for clarification. Applying them will require your own judgment. To aid you, we will reinforce the ideas with our personal experiences, stories, analogies, and examples from the Marine Corps, businesses, and education.

To also aid you in your understanding, and in response to General Gray's long-standing belief that you should "tell them what you are going to tell them, tell them, and then tell them again," we developed the chart on page 73 as a visual summary of Chapters 5 to 10. This is also consistent with our statement in the first Prologue about retention being greatly increased when you can think of ideas and concepts in plain, even visual, terms.

Do you also remember the criticism in the first Prologue about how many books about leadership never define leadership? *Warfighting* clearly defines leadership. And we begin our discussion of the higher levels of leadership with the Marines' view of leadership as our foundation and, in doing so, establish what Marines refer to as the end state (a concept we will discuss later).

> "Leadership is the personal ability to influence the performance of human beings in pursuit of a goal. The result of strong leadership is increased understanding and commitment from members of the organization."
>
> FMFM 1–1 *Campaigning*[12]

"Leaders must have a strong sense of the great responsibility of their office." (45) Some see a leader's position to be one of prestige, bringing with it certain rights and privileges, but we view leadership as a responsibility for the resources entrusted to the leader. Your most important resource is your people. Leadership begins with the relationship between the leader and the follower and leadership occurs when the leader places the needs of the follower first. A selfless

Vantage Leadership				
Chapter	Higher Levels of Leadership Themes		Concepts *(from Warfighting)*	Applied
5	Seeing the Possible over the Probable		*attrition thinking* *maneuver thought process*	being opportunistic
6	Staying Focused Despite Uncertainty	building momentum	*concentration* *speed (velocity and tempo)* *surprise* *boldness*	organizing for momentum
7		without creating certainty	*friction* *uncertainty* *fluidity* *disorder*	exploiting opportunities
8	Remaining Conceptual	in conflict	*Philosophy of command (implicit communications)* *commander's intent* *decision making*	judgment
9		end state planning	*focus of effort* *shaping the situation (spheres of interest and influence)* *mission tactics*	campaign planning (exercises, critiques)
10	Having Commitment and a Sense of Presence	courage/resolve passion values/culture		professional education
		in time and place selflessness		all or none?

leader recognizes that everything that is accomplished is done through people.

The Marine Corps "requires intelligent leaders with a penchant for boldness and initiative down to the lowest levels." (45) You may start with a vision, but unless leaders at all levels in an organization can see, as well as share in, the end state, the vision (the possible) will only remain a dream. "Boldness is an essential moral trait in a leader." (45) Moral relates to a belief in right and wrong. It is this moral compass that is reinforced by the leader's sense of responsibility. "Initiative, the willingness to act on one's own judgment, is a prerequisite for boldness." (45) Being bold in thought alone does not equate to a higher level of leadership—that requires action, and taking action boldly, requires initiative.

Acting boldly and with initiative in exercising one's judgment requires a willingness to make mistakes, as well as the acceptance of mistakes, at all levels. At higher levels of leadership, "errors . . . stemming from overboldness are a necessary part of learning. We should deal with such errors leniently; there must be no 'zero defects' mentality." (45) The key is in remaining conceptual. Remember, to us, conceptual is a way of thinking based on a leader's philosophy—and is defined as a system of ideas and a sum of ideals (personal convictions).

"Not only must we not stifle boldness, or initiative, we must continue to encourage both traits in spite of mistakes." (45) You might think this is in conflict with the introduction of "moral," a belief in right or wrong, in the above paragraph. Is it? The answer lies in where the emphasis is placed. In a search for certainty, a manager may emphasize a zero defects mentality in execution. To a manager, mistakes create uncertainty, which should be avoided. To a leader with a sense of great responsibility and a penchant for boldness and initiative, mistakes still create uncertainty, but uncertainty is viewed as a necessary step in seeing the possible. To a leader, the moral compass points to right or wrong, not in execution, but in the conceptual—living and leading based on ideals and ideas.

Some managers, seeking certainty, confuse "is it right" with "is it legal?" A decision consistent with the law should represent a minimum threshold for being right (in execution), but may not always lead to the right (conceptual) decision. To us, right goes beyond the (minimum) legal decision, to the conceptual (right based on our ideals and ideas). To a leader, being right frequently requires being bold and taking the initiative, while a manager may be content with turning the decisions over to others.

As a result, "we should deal severely with errors of inaction or timidity." (45) The failure to take action is, in itself, a decision—a decision not to act. It is your "duty to take initiative as the situation demands." (45) In presenting the idea of a higher level of leadership without reference to hierarchy, we have purposely brought the potential for leadership to every individual, at every level. In the Marines, initiative is a duty, but it can only be a duty in an environment where it is encouraged in spite of the mistakes (in execution) that can result. Creating that environment is both a requirement for, and a result of, leadership

"Consequently, trust is an essential trait among leaders." (45) You might say this is obvious given any definition of leadership that includes a relationship between a leader and a follower in the accomplishment of a goal. Clearly, a relationship cannot be built on distrust. But the obvious and the clear do not always result in reality. There are two important ideals: "Trust must be earned." (45) and "Trust is a product of confidence and familiarity." (45) Lasting trust doesn't come with a title, an office, or a uniform. Even if people initially grant trust to a person in a uniform, or a leader's position, it can quickly be lost if it isn't earned. And like interest, it must accrue on a daily basis.

"Confidence . . . results from demonstrated professional skill." (45) And like trust, confidence goes both ways. The follower gains confidence in the leader when professionalism is displayed and the leader builds confidence in the follower by personally observing their professional skills. "Familiarity results from shared experiences and a common philosophy." (45) Familiarity goes beyond observing to sharing, both experiences and philosophy. Think about it. People like people who like what they like. You bond with people through shared experiences and philosophies. To a manager focused on the task, time is not to be wasted. To a leader focused on the relationship, spending time with and listening to the people you are responsible for is an investment.

And when sharing experiences and philosophy remember (again obvious, but worth stating)—"Relationships among all leaders—should be based on honesty and frankness." (46) Wasn't it Mark Twain who said something like, *I'm not smart enough to lie. It would require remembering what I told each person.* Think about people who tell people what they think they want to hear. Sooner, or later, people get together and compare answers. The "worst-case scenario" is when someone who is responsible for other people (in this case we won't use the term leader) is unwilling, or afraid, to tell people when and how they are not performing. This lack of frankness frequently means the person is not given the opportunity to improve. Unfortunately, this can doom a person, or even an organization.

The need for frankness goes both ways. "Until a (leader) has reached and stated a decision, each subordinate should consider it his duty to provide his honest, professional opinion, even though it may be in disagreement." (46) Some might say the people they work with are unwilling to provide their opinions, or if they do, they seldom disagree. A quick response might be that you get the behavior you reward, or tolerate, but it would be better to return to the ideal stated above that leadership is a great responsibility and add that (leaders) "must encourage candor among (followers). Ready compliance . . . the behavior of "yes men" will not be tolerated." (46)

What about when a decision is supported in a meeting, only to be followed by a person or groups of individuals working against its implementation? "Once the decision has been reached, the junior then must support it as if it were his own." (46) Sometimes encouraging candor is not adequate for people who lack the courage to implement difficult decisions (even if they are their own). These are what we would call "flow-through" managers, not leaders. To them every statement has an owner other than themselves. Decisions are communicated to others as "someone else says," and input is stated as "someone else thinks." Sooner or later other people realize you can remove the flow-through manager with little, or no, loss to the organization.

By describing the end state, leadership as defined by and described in *Warfighting*, we have provided you a taste of what's to come—the idea of a higher level of leadership (Vantage) discussed through the themes of seeing the possible over the probable, staying focused despite uncertainty, remaining conceptual, and being committed.

Vantage Leadership				
Chapter	Higher Levels of Leadership Themes		Concepts *(from Warfighting)*	Applied
5	Seeing the Possible over the Probable		*attrition thinking* *maneuver thought process*	being opportunistic
6	Staying Focused Despite Uncertainty	building momentum	*concentration* *speed (velocity and tempo)* *surprise* *boldness*	organizing for momentum
7		without creating certainty	*friction* *uncertainty* *fluidity* *disorder*	exploiting opportunities
8	Remaining Conceptual	in conflict	*Philosophy of command (implicit communications)* *commander's intent* *decision making*	judgment
9		end state planning	*focus of effort* *shaping the situation (spheres of interest and influence)* *mission tactics*	campaign planning (exercises, critiques)
10	Having Commitment and a Sense of Presence	courage/ resolve passion values/culture		professional education
		in time and place selflessness		all or none?

CHAPTER FIVE

Vantage Leadership—Seeing the Possible

The difference between the probable and the possible can be most clearly seen through a discussion of two distinct styles of warfare—attrition and maneuver, as described in *Warfighting*. Are we comparing war to leadership? No. But war, with its inherent uncertainty and chaos, creates an environment where leadership is often born, frequently developed, and very often the secret to success. By drawing from this environment and the lessons learned both in war and in the preparation for it, you can be a better leader. Trust us and we think you will quickly see how a maneuver (not an attrition) philosophy is the key to seeing the possible (and being opportunistic) in any organization.

In a simplistic view, "an attrition style seeks victory through superior power and technology." (28) It relies on a Supreme Commander to tell the troops where and when to direct superior firepower. The key concept is power. The attritionist believes there is strength in numbers (size). Because massed firepower is costly, however, "the focus is on efficiency, leading to a methodical, almost scientific approach" (28) and a reliance on internal procedures and processes. "With the emphasis on the efficient application of the massed . . . movement tends to be ponderous and tempo relatively unimportant." (28) Much time can be incurred passing information up a "chain of command" and waiting for a decision to be sent down.

"The desire for volume and accuracy . . . tends to lead toward centralized control, just as the emphasis on efficiency tends to lead to an inward focus on procedures and techniques." (28) As a result, under attrition thinking there is little opportunity to take initiative or improvise. "Results are generally proportionate to efforts; greater expenditures net greater results—that is, greater attrition." (28) "The greatest necessity for success is numerical superiority Victory does not depend so much on . . . competence as on sheer superiority of numbers in men and equipment." (29) Not surprisingly, since the United States has maintained an overwhelming numerical and technological superiority, we have historically waged war by attrition.

In Chapter 2, comparisons were made between the second wave themes discussed and the actions of businesses during the industrial period. You might find it interesting to reread that discussion, inserting the attrition style of thinking, or the attritionist, whenever appropriate. We know you will find great similarities. Size is one example. There is a perceived strength in size. In the attrition style, strength in war (size) results from the number of assets and superior firepower. In business, size results in mass production and advertising.

The attritionist and business manager both attempt to create certainty. Both use structure in an attempt to control, which in turn slows communication. Decision making to the attritionist and the "second wave" manager is ponderous (as much time is spent waiting on others). To both, power is paramount. Neither approach encourages innovation or initiative. Can you see the resemblances?

Does this mean that the attritionists and business managers who followed the second wave industrial models were wrong? No! Looking back, the attrition style of warfare has generally been successful. Our country and our allies have enjoyed great superiority in technology and in numbers. Likewise, our businesses have been superior world leaders. Looking forward, however, we believe an entirely new approach, based on a different way of thinking, is needed.

Today's military has been shifting from a focus on attrition to a maneuver style of warfare. Maneuver itself is not new, however. Many of the concepts were described by Sun Tzu in the *Art of War*. But *Warfighting* took maneuver to a new, higher level. It developed a new philosophy, a doctrine, a thought process based on the concepts, characteristics, and principles of maneuver.

How does maneuver differ from the attrition style? "A maneuver style stems from a desire to circumvent a problem and attack it from a position of advantage. While attrition is based on power, by 'definition, maneuver relies on speed and surprise.' Based on movement, maneuver is clearly opportunistic. The need for speed in turn requires decentralized control. Decisions are made at the level closest to the point of action by those most informed. Tempo itself is a weapon—often the most important." (29)

Efficiency is replaced by exploiting opportunities. Reducing costs can still be important, but maneuver also emphasizes opportunities. In business, this could mean increasing revenues by exploiting opportunities. In the attrition style, success is measured by superiority in physical assets, as reflected in numbers and size. "To win by maneuver, we cannot substitute numbers for skill. Maneuver thus makes a greater demand on . . . judgment." (29) To succeed by reliance on speed and opportunities promotes an internal sense of pride and motivation.

Achievement fuels further achievement. In the Marines' maneuver thought process, the focus is on individual initiative, responsibility, and judgment. Because of the emphasis on speed, there is little time to wait for a decision from the "chain of command." Leadership is provided before a decision is made by establishing intent. Through training and education, risk is reduced as the individual is well prepared to take the initiative. A "been there, done that" attitude provides the individual with a sense of confidence to take responsibility. Leaders are confident that their intent will be carried out, even if only one person is left to complete the mission.

"Potential success by maneuver—unlike attrition—is often disproportionate to the effort made. But for exactly the same reasons, maneuver incompetently applied carries with it a greater chance for catastrophic failure, while attrition is inherently less risky." (29)

The risk needs further emphasis. As noted above, in maneuver we cannot substitute numbers for competency. Maneuver places greater demands on individual judgment. Unlike attrition, which can be led by a Supreme Commander, a maneuver thought process mandates that each leader and follower understand and be able to apply the concepts.

As we develop the concepts and characteristics of maneuver and describe how to prepare for a new way of thinking based on maneuver, it is critical that you consider the people in your organization. Success by maneuver thinking relies on both the judgment of the leader and the follower. You must have or build a trust in and understanding of the people you lead and follow, along with developing their understanding of the maneuver concepts.

Like the attrition style and the second wave themes, comparisons can be made between the maneuver way of thinking, the knowledge worker, and today's Judgment Revolution. Many businesses today recognize that speed is no longer a competitive advantage, but a requirement to "play the game." Smaller firms and often start-up firms have taken major corporations by surprise, capitalizing on the larger companies' inability to react quickly. In addition, the number of small businesses is growing at an increasing rate. People no longer see the large corporation as the lifetime employer. Today, every business is at risk, and there are few, if any, "blue-chip" stocks that are guaranteed to be supreme in the future.

Results are no longer solely quantitative. People are recognized as being more and more important to the success of a business. People movements, especially in high-tech firms, have almost instantly changed a company's value. Accountants, long the recorders of corporate history, are now looking for ways to reflect people as assets on a firm's balance sheet. Superiority in physical assets (based on numbers) is becoming a weakness in many industries. Consider banking. Not that long ago, the bank with the most branches was superior. Now, too many traditional branches can be a disadvantage. Technology has reduced the size of branches as ATMs and smaller customer convenience centers have been created based on new technology.

All businesses are recognizing the importance of time (speed) to their busy customers. Shop at home services (catalogue, cable TV, and Internet sales) are growing at increasing rates. The emphasis is on the customer. Mass advertising (the "firepower" of large corporations) is now being shifted to one-to-one, relationship-oriented marketing approaches. All businesses talk in terms of "niche," often looking for new advantages.

When we began our discussion of attrition and maneuver we asked you to trust us and you would learn how a maneuver philosophy is key to seeing the possible, while the attritionist is bound by the probable. Hopefully, the above examples have shown you how these two distinct styles of warfare represent different ways of thinking that are evident in any organizational setting. To the individual these are two separate ways of thinking, but like the waves of change, both attrition and maneuver thinking can be occurring at the same time within an organization, thus adding to the conflict faced by today's leader.

Wait a minute, you might be saying. Do you need to "enlist" in the Marines to reach the higher levels of leadership? Of course not, our intent is not to make you proficient in the styles of warfare, but to provide you with key ideas from a maneuver philosophy that you can rely on in developing your own opportunistic—seeing the possible—approach to the higher levels of leadership. Maneuver thinking is, in our opinion, a great example of how it can be done. However, it is not the only example of learning to see things in a different way, which is a precursor to seeing the possible over the probable.

Here is another example. In Franklin University's Leadership Philosophy class, students find leadership in books not normally thought to be about leadership. How is this accomplished? Relying on the works of DeBono (vertical versus lateral thinking) and Buzan[13] (mind mapping), students learn to identify leadership concepts (vertical thinking), but suspend the ordering (lateral thinking) of the ideas and ideals, then use the concept of mind mapping to order them in a new way, creating a leadership philosophy. In essence, they learn to see the possible over the probable (the written word).

Do you need to take the Leadership class at Franklin to learn how to reach the higher levels of leadership? Again, of course, the answer is no. Perhaps a couple of applied examples will help. Brian Gallagher, now President of United Way of America, changed the way of thinking of the Columbus, Ohio, United Way when he was its

President by asking the question "who is the customer?" The response he got was "the agencies we fund" (the probable). Brian changed the organization's way of thinking as he led them to realize the customer is the donor (the possible).

Likewise, Frank Yanchak, Franklin's Registrar, altered his department's way of thinking by shifting the "focus of main effort" (a concept we will explore later in depth) from keeping student records (the traditional registrar's role) and supporting three graduations a year (typically viewed as an extra burden), to seeing the possible. Now, the graduations are the focus of main effort (supported by keeping accurate records). Under Frank's leadership, students have completed their coursework as late as Saturday and still have received their diplomas at Sunday's graduation. After all, why would Frank's department want to spoil the graduation celebration of any student?

Although there are many other examples in support of the individual higher level of leadership themes—seeing the possible over the probable, staying focused despite uncertainty, remaining conceptual, and having commitment—we believe the concepts and the philosophy found in *Warfighting* represent the most comprehensive and pervasive example of all of the themes and will continue to advance this way of thinking as a new model for leadership. We must also warn you that learning the concepts will not only develop your philosophy for leading, but may change your way of thinking to become more like the Marines (in our opinion, an opportunity).

"The ability to take advantage of opportunity is a function of speed, flexibility, boldness, and initiative." (34) We will explore these ideas and other maneuver concepts in greater detail in the next chapters. In doing so, we hope you will gain not only a greater appreciation for the concepts, but also develop an understanding of how the concepts move across the higher level of leadership themes to create a new way of thinking. Are you prepared to take the next step and move to the next theme—staying focused despite uncertainty (without creating certainty) while building momentum?

Vantage Leadership				
Chapter	Higher Levels of Leadership Themes		Concepts *(from Warfighting)*	Applied
5	Seeing the Possible over the Probable		*attrition thinking* *maneuver thought process*	being opportunistic
6	Staying Focused Despite Uncertainty	building momentum	*concentration* *speed (velocity and tempo)* *surprise* *boldness*	organizing for momentum
7		without creating certainty	*friction* *uncertainty* *fluidity* *disorder*	exploiting opportunities
8	Remaining Conceptual	in conflict	*Philosophy of command (implicit communications)* *commander's intent* *decision making*	judgment
9		end state planning	*focus of effort* *shaping the situation (spheres of interest and influence)* *mission tactics*	campaign planning (exercises, critiques)
10	Having Commitment and a Sense of Presence	courage/resolve passion values/culture		professional education
		in time and place selflessness		all or none?

CHAPTER SIX

Vantage Leadership—Staying Focused—Building Momentum

Let's begin by summarizing our progress so far. In the first four chapters, we presented the waves of change and the revolutions. In Chapter 5 we introduced you to a new model for leadership, a higher level of leadership, based on the philosophy (way of thinking) found in *Warfighting*. In our discussion of the first higher level of leadership theme—seeing the possible over the probable—we focused on two different ways of thinking, attrition and maneuver.

We finished Chapter 5 by assuring you we would explore the concepts from a maneuver approach in greater detail as we turn our attention to staying focused despite uncertainty (without creating certainty) while building momentum. Once again, we will begin with the end state—building momentum (sustained speed) and its underlying concepts: concentration, speed (velocity and tempo), surprise, and boldness. Lastly, we will apply the concepts in our discussion of organizing for momentum. We then will be prepared to discuss in Chapter 7 staying focused in spite of uncertainty by adding the concepts of friction, fluidity, and disorder and how these concepts contribute to exploiting opportunities.

"Concentration and speed are two concepts of such significance and universality that we can advance them as principles." (31) You may have thought about the importance of speed in today's chaotic world, but the concept of concentration may represent a new idea, at least as it relates to leadership. It might be helpful to think of concentration as the maneuver response to time management (second wave) or managing the time resource (an updated approach). "Concentration is the convergence of effort in time and space." (31)

"The willingness to concentrate at the decisive place and time necessitates strict economy and the acceptance of risk elsewhere and at other times." (31) Often people fail to realize that committing resources to a place or a time means they may not be available for other opportunities that may arise. In attrition, resources are often concentrated where they will yield the greatest efficiencies or mass (power). And once committed, it is difficult, if not impossible (due to a controlling structure) to shift them.

But, at higher levels of leadership resources may be held in reserve, and then specifically allocated, or readily reallocated for opportunities. For example, Franklin University budgets a percentage of its endowment as an "entrepreneurial fund" to be used in support of new ideas and initiatives. By having a separate source of funding, Franklin can pursue new opportunities without taking resources from (annual) operations. Ask yourself if an opportunity were to arise, could you, or would your organization be able to concentrate the needed resources?

"To devote means to unnecessary efforts or excessive means to necessary secondary efforts violates the principle of concentration and is counterproductive to the true objective." (31) This is the key difference between setting priorities (time management) and allocating the appropriate level of resources to priorities (managing the time resource). Armed with this principle, we can return to our discussion (in Chapter 3) of rightsizing as an example of applying the concept of concentration.

Rightsizing has been used as a way to reduce excessive resources that have been allowed to build over time. If you apply it primarily as an efficiency technique, however, there is a tendency to make cuts "across the board," use a percentage for each area, eliminate open positions, or "freeze" hiring. The remaining fewer people may then be expected to accomplish everything previously completed under the same, or even faster, timelines. This is a second wave approach with the true objective being reducing resources (efficiency).

In a maneuver way of thinking, to apply the concept of concentration you would begin by identifying and eliminating resources that are being applied to unnecessary efforts. At the same time, you would remove excessive resources applied to necessary tasks. Tasks not directed at achieving a decisive advantage would be deferred, an example of concentrating resources in time. Resources freed up could then be reallocated. If the true objective is to concentrate resources at the desired place and time, not just downsizing, a "true right size" would be determined that could be either smaller or larger, depending on opportunities.

"We must concentrate not only at the decisive location, but also at the decisive moment." (31) We have all heard that timing is everything, and it is equally true in leadership. If you fail to act at the right moment, fleeting opportunities can pass you by. And when you act, you must do so with speed. Remember, maneuver relies on speed.

"Speed is the rapidity of action. Like concentration, speed applies to both time and space. And like concentration, it is *relative* speed that matters." (32) To gain a decisive advantage, you must move faster than your competition. In today's businesses, everyone seems to be talking about the need to move fast. Even huge second wave companies can generate bursts of speed, but sooner or later their size and excessive policies and procedures will slow or even stop their movement. Speed allows you to capture the initiative. Remember that more than one person was working on inventing the telephone, but Alexander Graham Bell brought it to market first and captured the initiative.

"Speed over time is tempo—the consistent ability to operate fast. Speed over distance, or space, is velocity—the ability to move fast. Since it is relative speed that matters, it follows that we should take all measures to improve our own tempo and velocity." (32) Relative speed can create an advantage, but tempo is critical to seizing and maintaining the initiative. How many times have you seen a successful new project lead to requests for more and more resources to sustain (or defend) the competitive advantage? Adding resources often leads to more structure, procedures, and complexity resulting in reduced velocity and tempo, and your advantage of relative speed is lessened or lost.

Today the decisive advantage belongs to those who are more "fit" (leaner, with less bureaucracy) and can operate consistently faster than others. But, no matter how "fit" an individual or an organization is, there must be periods of lesser activity to allow for "rest and relaxation." "Experience shows that we cannot sustain a high rate of velocity or tempo indefinitely." (32) Failure to understand the need for people to recharge their energies will greatly reduce an organization's ability to "push to the limit" when it is required. In addition, pushing people when it is not required can greatly limit their willingness to respond when it is needed. If you wish to seize and maintain initiative through tempo you must provide for, and encourage, people to engage in periods of reduced activity.

"Speed provides security." (32) In times of great change, it is natural for you to feel less secure. Your fears may be magnified when fellow workers, friends, or family members have also felt the negative results associated with change (such as downsizing). Some may wish they could return to the feelings of safety associated with working for one of the large industrial corporations created during the second wave. But in today's global marketplace these companies, often because of their size and rigidity, are less secure.

Speed creates a new security by providing the opportunity to take an offensive position, causing others, no matter how large they are, to react to your actions. Sitting back and waiting, or following those who take the initiative, are reactions subject to great risk. Security no longer takes the form of seniority (time in place) but is created by being ready, willing, and able to create an advantage through the effective use of velocity and tempo (speed).

"The combination of concentration and speed is momentum. Momentum generates impetus." (32) From the above discussion, you can see the complexity of momentum. It brings together the concepts we have discussed, but it is much more than being the quickest (velocity), or even sustaining speed over time (tempo). Nor is working harder and faster (more speed alone) the same as creating momentum. Applying excessive resources to sustain speed may give the impression of momentum, but it violates the concept of concentration in space. And sustained speed (tempo), applied to a lower priority project, defeats the purpose of concentrating resources in time. To achieve momentum requires your understanding of these principles, their interrelationships, and your ability to apply them in seizing the initiative.

Unfortunately, it is easier to find examples of failures in achieving momentum than successes. If you are not careful, your quest for speed alone can cause you to lose your concentration, and may leave many of your people behind (physically or mentally), thus reducing the resources available. You may also restrict people's ability to move with speed due to how much they have to "carry." People who are overburdened with unnecessary tasks cannot move quickly or sustain their pace. As a result, responding to the next opportunity takes longer than before.

Fortunately, there is an excellent way to determine if you are maintaining momentum. It's called OODA Loop. It is based on the pioneering concepts of retired Air Force Colonel John Boyd, a disciple of Sun Tzu's philosophy.[14] OODA stands for Observation, Orientation, Decision, and Action. In Boyd's theory, a party in conflict first observes the situation. Then on the basis of that observation, orients himself, meaning he takes in the totality of the situation. Next he makes a decision which he then implements—takes action. Taking action creates a new situation, which begins the loop all over again. Boyd proposed that among the parties involved in a conflict, whichever one consistently completes the cycle faster gains the advantage (maintains the momentum).

Does the OODA Loop apply to your business? We think it does. Consider any initiative. Learning from its implementation, will you complete the cycle quicker the next time? If not, someone else (a competitor) can and you will ultimately lose the momentum. The relative advantage belongs to whoever consistently completes the OODA Loop faster.

Like concentration and speed, surprise and boldness are two additional maneuver concepts that increase your ability to take advantage of opportunity and build momentum. "Surprise means doing the unexpected thing, which in turn normally means doing the more difficult thing in hopes that (others) will not expect it. Purposely choosing the more difficult course because it is less expected necessarily means sacrificing efficiency to some degree." (33)

Surprise does not require you catching someone unaware, but only that the other side becomes aware at a time they cannot react effectively. Beyond the obvious advantages, surprise can be a multiplier because of its psychological effects. There is a natural comfort in doing the same thing repeatedly. By your doing the unexpected, surprise can be created. In today's changing business climate, focusing on the easiest, most efficient course of action frequently results in lost opportunities. Choosing the more difficult action creates risk, but in the long-term can provide you with psychological as well as economic advantages.

There are numerous examples of businesses that are successful because they do the unexpected, often the more difficult, or less efficient. Creating a product that others may see as less "glamorous" is one example. Providing a product in fewer quantities, but with higher quality is another. Exploiting an opportunity may come from your doing something in a new way that adds value to the product or service. Another example is the smaller start-up companies that are able to get to the market quicker, relying on speed to create a competitive advantage.

However, "its advantages are only temporary and must be quickly exploited." (34) Creating a market position by speed alone may be difficult for you to defend in the long run. It is important to realize that some advantages may not be economically feasible because the position may be lost before there is a sufficient return. This does not diminish the importance of surprise. There are times when surprise is so important to establishing a position that others can never overcome it (inventions are an example). And in all situations, you having the element of surprise will always be an advantage over being surprised by your competitors.

Unlike other maneuver concepts, surprise does not solely depend on your own efforts. Achieving surprise depends on the expectations of others. They may not be expecting you to do the most difficult thing. Surprise also rests on the level of preparedness of others.

As a result, beyond being difficult to achieve, surprise quickly dissipates as others become aware of your actions. Therefore, speed is critical in both creating surprise and exploiting the opportunities that result. Further, creating surprise is frequently aided by the concept of boldness.

"Boldness is superior to timidity in every instance and it is at a disadvantage only in the face of nervy, calculating patience . . . a form of boldness in its own right." (34) Boldness is closely related to surprise, and to quickly seize the advantage of surprise often requires boldness. While waiting can (in some situations) be an act of boldness, a propensity toward action can also be a significant multiplier. In business, boldness most often takes the form of doing what others are not—being a leader instead of a follower. As a result, boldness almost always involves increased risk. But there is also great risk in not acting boldly. "Boldness must be tempered by judgment lest it border on recklessness. But this does not diminish its significance." (34)

Boldness, like surprise, can often be achieved by taking the more difficult course of action. In business, mistakes can also be opportunities to demonstrate boldness. Your quick and decisive response (beyond that expected by the customer) to correct a problem can often turn around a negative situation. In the reverse, unwillingness to correct a mistake because someone is afraid to admit an error can result in major (customer relations) damage. To fail to take a difficult course of action because the customers would see that you are wrong is an absurdity. The customer knows you are wrong and is waiting (impatiently) to see if you have the boldness to correct it.

> *"Kill Complacency—before it kills you. In this competitive age, today's leaders need to know how to blow up self-satisfied corporate cultures. One hint: Create a sense of urgency before a disaster strikes."*
>
> John P. Kotter[16]

Surprise and boldness can be effective weapons against complacency. It is often said that success builds complacency. Doing things the same way leads to a lack of innovation, surprise, and boldness. It is natural to not see new things if you only follow well-established paths. Consider your drive to work. If you follow the same roads every day, it is highly unlikely you will see anything new. Often you will even have a delayed reaction to changes that are occurring in front of you. You have become complacent. Try being bold, taking a new route. You might find some surprises, as well as opportunities.

Through our discussion of the concepts of boldness, surprise, speed, and concentration, we hope you have developed a better understanding of momentum (sustained speed). As we have already stated, staying focused despite uncertainty (without creating certainty) while building momentum (sustained speed) may appear simple on the surface, but there is a tremendous complexity to this theme. Momentum can be difficult to achieve and sustain because of the interrelationship of concentration and speed, applied in the dimensions of both space and time. The key is in how well people, both leaders and followers, can work together effectively, concentrating resources and using speed to create momentum.

Sustaining momentum requires the ultimate team effort. Momentum clearly requires judgment. It is difficult to imagine a second, or even a third wave organization maintaining or even creating momentum. In today's Judgment Revolution, momentum can be a tremendous multiplier, greatly expanding our abilities to exploit opportunities. Not surprising, the Marines carry these concepts into how they are organized. Speed is the key outcome.

Your organization "must be capable of responding immediately" with "no standard structure" but one that is "appropriate for the specific situation." We "should streamline our headquarters, organizations and staffs to eliminate bureaucratic delays in order to add tempo." (42–43) In the second wave industrial era, businesses often followed standard structures, with hierarchical levels and line and staff positions. In today's world, organizational structures can no longer be standardized. The number of reporting levels has decreased in most businesses. People are being organized along product lines, types of customers, locations, or projects (to name just a few common ones). Teams that cross functional boundaries are often formed for specific projects. What's the right organization for your business? One that allows for a quick response to opportunities.

Does your organization support momentum? Or is control centralized, your "chain-of-command" never broken? Are bureaucratic delays common? Is there friction between units and the rest of the organization? A non-scientific but useful test is to listen to how people speak about your organization. Do they talk in terms of "we" or "they?" If the discussion most often reflects a "they" mentality, people may fear uncertainty ("look what they are doing now"). If people speak as "we," they may be reflecting relationships and trust in their peers and leaders.

In maneuver thinking the human dimension is the key. Individuals must be able to think, take initiative and responsibility, accept accountability, and exercise judgment individually and in units. This requires operational familiarity. What does it mean? It means leaders at all levels "should establish habitual relationships between supported and supporting units to develop operational familiarity among those units. This does not preclude nonstandard relationships when required by the situation." (43)

Maintaining momentum requires developing a familiarity with your people. Knowing your people, their likes and dislikes, helps them function as a unit, improving momentum. Routinely establishing relationships lessens friction. Getting to know, in advance, the people who will be there to help you accomplish your objectives builds trust. Nonstandard structures are supported by trusting relationships. Developing an operational familiarity is what holds a unit together through uncertainty and allows structures to be improvised to fit the situation.

The Marines also apply maneuver thinking to their use of supporting resources. They guard against an overreliance on technology. Advantages from technology are seen as only temporary. Long-term results come from people. To sustain momentum, Marines want equipment to be easy to operate and maintain, reliable, and with minimal training required. In today's "high tech world," there will always be a tendency for some to want to solve all problems through technology. But technology is best viewed as a tool to be employed by people to gain momentum and exploit opportunities. Remember the credo: equip the man, not man the equipment.

Having discussed building momentum, supported by concentration, speed, surprise, and boldness, applied through organizing for momentum, we can now turn our attention in Chapter 7 to staying focused in spite of uncertainty.

Vantage Leadership				
Chapter	Higher Levels of Leadership Themes		Concepts *(from Warfighting)*	Applied
5	Seeing the Possible over the Probable		*attrition thinking* *maneuver thought process*	being opportunistic
6	Staying Focused Despite Uncertainty	building momentum	*concentration* *speed (velocity and tempo)* *surprise* *boldness*	organizing for momentum
7		without creating certainty	*friction* *uncertainty* *fluidity* *disorder*	exploiting opportunities
8	Remaining Conceptual	in conflict	*Philosophy of command (implicit communications)* *commander's intent* *decision making*	judgment
9		end state planning	*focus of effort* *shaping the situation (spheres of interest and influence)* *mission tactics*	campaign planning (exercises, critiques)
10	Having Commitment and a Sense of Presence	courage/ resolve passion values/culture		professional education
		in time and place selflessness		all or none?

CHAPTER SEVEN

Vantage Leadership—Staying Focused Despite Uncertainty

In Chapter 6 we began discussing our second higher level of leadership theme—staying focused despite uncertainty—with the end state of building momentum (sustained speed) and its underlying concepts of concentration, speed, surprise, and boldness. We then applied these concepts in organizing for momentum. We can now continue by adding friction, fluidity, and disorder, and discussing how these maneuver concepts impact both momentum and staying focused despite uncertainty.

Ultimately, we will discuss exploiting opportunities. Along the way, we continue building our new model for leadership based on the maneuver thought process—a model that is needed in today's chaotic, uncertain, complex, and changing world—a world that has created the Conflicted Leader.

Change is frequently met by resistance (friction) that is a natural reaction to the unknown (uncertainty). Maneuver is based on movement, and any movement, like change, creates friction and uncertainty. Your understanding of both change and friction is critical to generating momentum. If not mastered, they become strong forces working against momentum. Friction and uncertainty are natural outcomes of change in any setting. As you will see below, functioning at a higher level of leadership, staying focused in an environment of friction and uncertainty, will allow you to achieve and maintain greater momentum (without creating certainty).

In his classic book, *On War*, von Clausewitz described friction "as 'the force that makes the apparently easy so difficult.'[16] Friction is the force that resists all action. It makes the simple difficult and the difficult seemingly impossible." (4) In the maneuver way of thinking, friction is viewed as a natural phenomenon. It is accepted as a given. But your failure to understand it can lead to inappropriate responses that may increase friction. Your ability to seize the initiative can be greatly reduced by friction. Momentum requires speed. Friction reduces velocity. And as it has the potential to build as a reaction to movement (change), friction can also suppress tempo (speed over time). Although you can reduce unnecessary friction and limit its effects, it is your ability to function with friction, through an understanding of its many facets, which will allow you to create and sustain momentum.

"Friction may be mental, as in indecision over a course of action." (5) Physical obstacles may be the most easily understood, yet it is mental friction that is the most potentially damaging. Physical obstacles can often be seen, but mental friction is often buried. It can result from not making a decision as well as from failing to appropriately and timely implement a decision once it is made. In the extreme, mental friction can also take the form of "malicious obedience," following someone's directions, even though they are incomplete, or following the specific wording instead of the known intent.

"Friction may be external." (5) External friction is caused by situations outside your direct control. This could include the actions of other businesses, governmental laws or regulations, natural disasters, or random occurrences. "Friction may be self induced, caused by such factors as lack of a clearly defined goal, lack of coordination, unclear or complicated plans, complex task organization or command relationships, or complicated communication systems." (5) Self-induced, internal friction is friction in its most lethal form.

Knowing the underlying causes of friction (external or internal) can help you in understanding and responding to people's reactions. Viewing friction solely as people's resistance to any change fails to understand the impact of self-induced, internal friction. Are people resisting all change? Or do their actions result from self-induced friction? External friction may be reduced by such techniques as environmental scanning and scenario-based planning, but the greatest reduction in friction will come through your minimizing internal friction by setting clear goals, coordinating efforts, establishing plans, simplifying organizational relationships, and improving the way you communicate.

"While we should attempt to minimize self-induced friction, the greater requirement is to (lead) effectively within the medium of friction." (5) It is important to recognize that some amount of friction is inevitable. No matter how well you communicate, there may always be some people who resist any change (movement). Despite your intense communication efforts, some may never share your organization's goals. It has been said that in any situation there are some who will move forward whether or not there is leadership present. There are also some who will not move forward despite all your efforts. The rest will wait to see how you react to both groups.

Thus, to function effectively, your greater requirement is to prevail over the friction. "The means to overcome friction is the will; we will prevail over friction through persistent strength of mind and spirit." (5) There are numerous examples of businesses that are overcome by the effects of friction, but there are also organizations that carry on and accomplish goals in spite of their own limitations (friction). "We can readily identify countless examples of friction, but until we experience it ourselves, we cannot hope to appreciate it fully. Only through experience can we come to appreciate the force of will necessary to overcome friction and to develop a realistic appreciation for what is possible." (5)

How can you develop the will to overcome friction? In the Marines, the emphasis is on experience and training, a "been there, done that" attitude prevails. We have all experienced friction. It can be the resistance of others to your ideas, or your own resistance to the changes brought upon you by others. Only by experiencing friction can you learn the force of will necessary for you to overcome it and to develop your realistic appreciation for the possible. You may look at resistance to change as impeding your progress (and it may), but you should also accept that change, and the resistance to change, is a natural phenomena that impacts all people.

"Because we are involved in a human enterprise, whatever form friction takes it will always have a psychological as well as a physical impact." (5) People react to the sources of friction in different ways. When confronted with external friction, a catastrophe caused by factors considered outside the control of a business for example, there is often a willingness of people to pull together. As a result, the change becomes the common "enemy" and friction can be used as a rallying point. Some business leaders, although not necessarily welcoming a crisis, may use the situation to reduce complacency and create a sense of cohesion within the organization. Inversely, self-induced friction has a tendency to pull your people apart, reducing their capability to work together. Change becomes the antagonist. The key is for you to create a feeling of shared ownership by minimizing self-induced friction. In doing so, you will also reduce uncertainty.

Has all of this discussion so far led you to a feeling of too much uncertainty? We hope not. It is not our purpose. Our intent is to explain to you in greater depth the higher level leadership theme of staying focused in spite of uncertainty. Introducing new ideas, like any change, is in itself a natural source of uncertainty. "Uncertainty is just one of the many sources of friction, but because it is such a pervasive trait . . . we will treat it singly." (6)

Do you remember our discussion about the differences between management and leadership? We said we manage certainty, but leadership "takes place in the atmosphere of uncertainty." (6) Clausewitz called uncertainty "the fog of war." Fog is a great metaphor for it. Looking in the dictionary, you would find the words haze and daze used to define uncertainty. For our purposes, however, there is a difference. Our intent is for you to not let the haze (reduced vision) become the daze (a state of confusion). This is another way of saying—staying focused despite uncertainty.

"Uncertainty pervades in the form of unknowns—about the competition, about other external factors, and even about internal (friendly) factors." (restated 6) "While we try to reduce these unknowns by gathering information, we must realize we cannot eliminate them." (6) The key is in the realization that you must move forward without wasting resources by trying to create certainty. Managers, who want to live in a world of certainty, find themselves in a state of constant conflict trying to create a false sense of certainty through policies, rules, and procedures all wrapped up in a constant stream of memos, e-mail, and organizational structures and charts.

"The very nature of (leadership) makes absolute certainty impossible; all actions . . . will be based on incomplete, inaccurate, or even contradictory information." (6) In the second and third waves, business became too data driven. Computers allowed us to gather and manipulate data, often in a search for certainty. Computer reports may even create a false look of certainty to data that is inaccurate, incomplete, or contradictory. In today's world, the emphasis is on converting data to information, but the result will still not be certainty. In creating momentum, you cannot wait for a certainty that will never come. Instead, you learn to move forward, and act based on the information available (accepting the risks of the unknown).

"By its nature, uncertainty invariably involves the estimation and acceptance of risk. Risk is inherent and involved in every (situation)." (7) Business leaders have long understood and applied risk in decision making. In the second wave, they attempted to quantify and reduce risk. In a maneuver approach, however, taking a prudent risk may be a way of gaining the initiative. As already stated, concentrating resources, a key element of momentum, creates risk. Speed relies on rapid and sustained movement, and as a result, involves more risk than staying in place. The potential for greater gain requires the acceptance of more risk

While you cannot eliminate risk, you can mitigate it by considering the potential consequences of your actions under consideration. Risks can be acceptable or unacceptable, and the key is for you to learn the difference. For example, there may be great (financial) risk in moving forward with rapidly changing technology. But to wait until technology prices are substantially lower may allow others to take the initiative and gain the momentum. You may decide the financial risk is acceptable, while the loss of the initiative to a competitor is an unacceptable risk. Today, the greater risk results from not taking chances (acceptable risks). It is also good to remember, "risk is equally common to action and inaction." (7)

Along with the acceptance of risk, staying focused in spite of friction and uncertainty is aided by an understanding of the related maneuver concepts of fluidity and disorder. In Chapter Four, we proposed judgment as the fourth wave of change and uncertainty as the tide. Carrying the metaphor forward, we can add fluidity and disorder to represent the "current" that brings a sense of flow to our discussion of uncertainty. The idea of a flow may not seem readily applicable to leadership until you consider that "decisive results . . . are rarely the direct result of an initial, deliberate action. Rather the initial action creates the conditions for subsequent actions which develop from it." (37)

"Like friction and uncertainty, fluidity, is an integral attribute. Each episode . . . is the temporary result of the unique combination of circumstances, requiring an original solution. No episode can be viewed in isolation. Rather, each merges with those that precede and follow it—shaped by the former and shaping the conditions of the latter—creating a continuous, fluctuating fabric of activity replete with fleeting opportunities and unforeseen events." (7 and 8)

Unlike friction and uncertainty, which restrict your ability to achieve and sustain momentum, understanding fluidity can create conditions ripe for opportunities that you can exploit by unexpected and bold actions. But your actions are affected by many elements, including the people whom you will rely on to implement your decision, as well as those affected by it. The event itself is also a product of many factors, including all past actions and inactions, known and unknown, that created the situation. Equally important, but less certain, are the events that will follow your action. Understanding the characteristic of fluidity can greatly enhance your ability to create opportunities that can lead to decisive results.

Consider how the concept of fluidity supports Boyd's OODA Loop. He recognized that each action creates a new situation. Boyd's conclusion—the advantage belongs to the one who can consistently complete the OODA Loop faster. Likewise, the concept of fluidity concludes, "Success depends in large part on the ability to adapt to a constantly changing situation." (8)

In business, the characteristic of fluidity can be applied in multiple ways. Your understanding of fluidity can create a sense of continuity. In a rapidly changing environment, keeping your people informed is critical. But if you report only on seemingly isolated activities, people will not see how the output of one event can be the input to the next. Look at your meetings. Is each one seen in isolation? What about your reports? Consider how a sense of fluidity (continuity) could be achieved. Each meeting, or report, could begin with a summary of what was planned, followed by the results achieved, and ending with the plans for the next period. In this way, each individual would be better prepared to react to unforeseen circumstances and opportunities occurring between meetings or reports.

To the individual manager who is seeking certainty and thinking with an attrition mindset, each situation is often seen in isolation. To the leader following the maneuver thought process, there is an understanding that events have a sense of flow, a beginning, a current state, and a future impact. Likewise, those at higher levels of leadership have a realization of their position over time, holding an appreciation for those who came before, as well as an awareness that there will be others who will succeed them. We will explore this further in our discussion of a sense of presence in Chapter 10.

Like fluidity, "disorder is an integral characteristic . . . we can never eliminate it. In an environment of friction, uncertainty, and fluidity, disorder is natural." (restatement 8) "We cannot think of today's (world) in linear terms." (9) Looking back, it may have been possible in the past to describe situations in a more orderly, linear way. Life may have been simpler. But now each change in an individual situation, and over time, naturally and geometrically increases disorder.

"We cannot hope to impose precise, positive control over events." (9) In the past, the response to disorder was to try to establish control over situations. The desire to control events may be the underlying cause of a great amount of self-induced friction in business. Many individuals who seek a high degree of control from their managers (as well as the managers who provide it) may be consciously or subconsciously resisting the changes that are underway.

Someone once said, "The second quickest way to commit suicide in business is to not accept change, the quickest way is to resist change."

In the industrial period, the concept of "span of control" (the number of people a manager can supervise and control) was discussed and debated. Now, layers and layers of management have been eliminated, organizational structures flattened, and dual reporting relationships are commonplace. As a result, there is more disorder, and exerting positive control over people who may be on other floors, in other buildings, states, and countries is simply not possible.

"As the situation changes continuously, we are forced to improvise again and again until finally our actions have little if any resemblance to the original scheme." (9) There was a time in business when people may have worked at the same desk from the start of their career until retirement. Today, people are on the move even within their organizations, creating feelings of disorder. Efforts to get closer to the customer and cross-functional teams are only two of the reasons. Technology (voice mail, e-mail, Internet, and cellular phones) has also greatly expanded our ability to communicate from disparate locations and at all hours.

"The best we can hope for is to impose a general framework of order on the disorder, to prescribe the general flow of action rather than to control each event." (9 and 10) An analogy can be found in leadership. By "stepping back" and looking at the "big picture" the leader can see the forest instead of the trees. Likewise, by seeking order over the flow of action (the forest), not in individual events (trees), the leader can provide a framework for disorder. We will explore this in greater detail in the next chapter when we discuss the next higher level of leadership theme—remaining conceptual. But first we will apply the concepts discussed in this and the previous chapters in our discussion of exploiting opportunities.

"The ability to take advantage of opportunity is a function of speed, flexibility, boldness, and initiative. By exploiting opportunities, we create in increasing numbers more opportunities for exploitation. It is often the ability and the willingness to ruthlessly exploit these opportunities that generate decisive results." (37) Nowhere in

Warfighting do the Marines make any excuses for the use of the terms "exploiting" or "ruthless." So what follows is not offered as an excuse, but only as an explanation.

To some the term exploiting implies taking an "unfair" advantage. But, like most words, there are multiple definitions, including an "undertaking that requires boldness" and "a remarkable act." Likewise, ruthless means "unrelenting." In the military the use of these terms would seldom be questioned. Why did we choose to repeat them in a book about leadership? Because we believe as a leader today you must be unrelenting in your pursuit of seeing the possible over the probable. Likewise, we believe staying focused despite uncertainty while building momentum is a remarkable act that requires boldness. To use softer words would ignore the uncertainty that has been created by the multiple revolutions impacting today's Conflicted Leader. Like the concepts we have presented, the terms themselves are bold, opportunistic statements.

Being opportunistic is more than a single concept, principle, or idea. It is a critical component of the maneuver thought process. It is a way of looking at the same situation as others, but seeing the possible (identifying opportunities) and taking the initiative (exploiting opportunities) that others would not. In today's world, the ability to identify actions, inactions, and chance occurrences that can be ruthlessly exploited no longer rests in the minds of a relative few. Every individual has the potential to observe situations, make connections, and identify opportunities in any environment. Are you ready to take the initiative and exploit opportunities? If so, we can turn our focus to our next higher level of leadership theme—remaining conceptual as a way of thinking.

<table>
<tr><th colspan="5">Vantage Leadership</th></tr>
<tr><th>Chapter</th><th colspan="2">Higher Levels of Leadership Themes</th><th>Concepts
(from Warfighting)</th><th>Applied</th></tr>
<tr><td>5</td><td>Seeing the Possible over the Probable</td><td></td><td>*attrition thinking*
maneuver thought process</td><td>being opportunistic</td></tr>
<tr><td>6</td><td rowspan="2">Staying Focused Despite Uncertainty</td><td>building momentum</td><td>*concentration*
speed (velocity and tempo)
surprise
boldness</td><td>organizing for momentum</td></tr>
<tr><td>7</td><td>without creating certainty</td><td>*friction*
uncertainty
fluidity
disorder</td><td>exploiting opportunities</td></tr>
<tr><td>8</td><td rowspan="2">Remaining Conceptual</td><td>in conflict</td><td>*Philosophy of command (implicit communications)*
commander's intent
decision making</td><td>judgment</td></tr>
<tr><td>9</td><td>end state planning</td><td>*focus of effort*
shaping the situation (spheres of interest and influence)
mission tactics</td><td>campaign planning (exercises, critiques)</td></tr>
<tr><td rowspan="2">10</td><td rowspan="2">Having Commitment and a Sense of Presence</td><td>courage/resolve
passion
values/culture</td><td></td><td>professional education</td></tr>
<tr><td>in time and place
selflessness</td><td></td><td>all or none?</td></tr>
</table>

CHAPTER EIGHT

Vantage Leadership—Remaining Conceptual—The Conflicted Leader

You were introduced to a new model for leadership in the Second Prologue. Called Vantage Leadership, it is forged on a special foundation, the philosophy found in *Warfighting*. This new model underlies the higher level of leadership themes—seeing the possible over the probable, staying focused despite uncertainty, remaining conceptual, and being committed. Chapter 5 presented the maneuver way of thinking as the clearest example of seeing the possible over the probable. In Chapters 6 and 7 we continued uniting the themes with the philosophy by expanding on the concepts found in *Warfighting*.

We can now move from discussing these concepts to being conceptual. It is not a major shift. Looking back to the Introduction where the higher level of leadership themes were first presented, remaining conceptual was described as "a way of thinking based on a leader's philosophy. A leadership (not an academic) philosophy defined as a system of ideas and a sum of ideals (personal convictions). A leadership philosophy is best conveyed through intent and example."

The concepts that we have already discussed are part of a way of thinking, a philosophy as it is defined. To see this better, we can once again examine *Warfighting* to further understand its intent and examples. First published by the Marine Corps in 1989 as FMFM 1 *Warfighting*, it "does not contain specific techniques and procedures for conduct," providing instead "broad guidance in the form of concepts and values. It is the Marine Corps' doctrine . . . a philosophy for action . . . a way of thinking in general. It requires judgment in application." (Foreword) It was expected (and continues) to be read, reread, and understood by every Marine officer.

Warfighting further states the "challenge is to identify and adopt a concept . . . consistent with our understanding of the nature and theory . . . and the realities. . . . What exactly does this require? It requires a concept . . . that will function effectively in an uncertain, chaotic, and fluid environment. It requires a concept that is consistent across the full spectrum . . . because we cannot attempt to change our basic doctrine from situation to situation and expect to be proficient." (57) "The Marine Corps concept for winning under these conditions is a . . . doctrine based on rapid, flexible, and opportunistic maneuver." (58)

The Marine Corps answered their challenge with *Warfighting*. Likewise, we can answer your challenge by uniting the higher level of leadership theme—remaining conceptual in the face of increased conflict—with the guidance from *Warfighting*, epitomized in the maneuver concepts. As we have already discussed in Chapters 1 through 4, your conflict does not come from hostile action, but instead results from the clash of ideas across the waves of change and the resulting revolutions, all of which are impacting you, the Conflicted Leader, at the same time.

In this chapter, we discuss remaining conceptual in conflict with the broad guidance, a way of thinking based on a leader's philosophy found in the concepts of philosophy of command, commander's intent, and decision making. Through examples in both business and the military, we will show how you can apply them in today's Judgment Revolution.

In Chapter 9, we will continue our discussion of remaining conceptual, once again beginning with the end state. This time the end state is also a way of thinking—and we will discuss end state planning and the related ideas of focus of effort, shaping the situation, and mission tactics. We will then answer the challenge of how you can remain conceptual in an uncertain, chaotic, and fluid environment by presenting a system of ideas that is consistent across the full spectrum. This system is based on rapid, flexible, and opportunistic maneuver; the Marines call it campaign planning.

Let's first examine philosophy of command. To many, command is equated with control and giving orders. Those not familiar with today's military may still visualize the officer as one who barks out orders to be followed without thinking by the troops. This perception is consistent with command in an attrition style, where superiority is the basis for control. In a maneuver way of thinking, command is much more. It means taking command and accepting the responsibility for other people, as well as the situation. A maneuverist uses command not to control, but to exploit opportunities. Philosophy of command is consistent with the maneuver thought process because it recognizes the impact of the changing situation and the uncertainty that results.

"First and foremost, in order to generate the tempo . . . we desire and to best cope with the uncertainty, disorder, and fluidity, command must be decentralized." (62) Leaders, at all levels, "must make decisions on their own initiative, based on their understanding of commander's intent (discussed below), rather than passing information up the chain of command and waiting for the decision to be passed down." (62) Philosophy of command and decentralized execution are based on the belief that someone "who is at the point of a decision will naturally have a better appreciation for the true situation than a senior some distance removed. Individual initiative and responsibility are of paramount importance." (62)

"Second, since we have concluded that . . . no amount of technology can reduce the human dimension, our philosophy of command must be based on human characteristics rather than on equipment or procedures. Our philosophy must not only accommodate but must exploit human traits such as boldness, initiative, personality, strength of will, and imagination. Our philosophy of command must also exploit the human ability to communicate implicitly." (62) The idea of implicit communication is especially applicable in today's Judgment Revolution. With so much information available, many conclude that the lack of effective communication is the source of many problems in today's businesses despite the considerable resources organizations spend on their communication efforts.

Because change is occurring at an ever-increasing rate and uncertainty flows from change, internal communications—keeping people informed—has become a major priority. Yet one communication survey after another reports that people still feel out of the communication loop (a source of internal friction). "We believe that implicit communication—to communicate through mutual understanding, using a minimum of key, well-understood phrases or even anticipating each other's thoughts—is a faster, more effective way to communicate than through the use of detailed, explicit instructions." (63)

The best example of implicit communications may be a well-trained hockey team as they advance toward their opponent's goal. Moving at lightning speed there is no time to stop and talk. Instead they seem to know almost instinctively where the other players are, or will be. The very best players pass the puck to a seemingly open spot with the confidence of knowing that their teammate will be there. How can you develop such an instinct? "We develop this ability through familiarity and trust, which are based on a shared philosophy and shared experience. This concept has several practical implications." (63)

"First, we should establish long-term working relationships to develop the necessary familiarity and trust." (63) The time to establish relationships and the trust that develops is not when a problem arises, but before—well before. "Our philosophy also requires familiarity . . . because only through a shared understanding can we develop the implicit communications necessary for unity of effort." (65) The values and culture that develop this trust and familiarity will be explored in greater detail in our discussion of commitment in Chapter 10.

"Second, key people—'actuals'—should talk directly to one another when possible, rather than through communicators or messengers." (63) Those who see a leader's position as a right and not a responsibility are the ones most likely to put up barriers (gatekeepers) between themselves and their people. For leadership, the old saying "don't kill the messenger" might become "kill the messenger" and talk directly to your people. It develops relationships and trust.

"Third, we should communicate orally when possible, because we communicate also in how we talk; our inflections and tone of voice." (63) The good news is that voice mail and e-mail have greatly reduced the stacks of memos from the past. The bad news is that the

Internet has made it easy to communicate with people by e-mail, even when they sit across from us. For those who lack courage, e-mail has become a preferred way to deliver bad news.

"And fourth, we should communicate in person when possible, because we communicate also through our gestures and bearing." (63) Not every message requires a personal visit. Confirming a meeting, submitting expected data, a quick and simple response, or even communicating when one party is out of the office (to be followed-up with a face-to-face discussion, if needed) are a few examples of the effectiveness of e-mail. But whenever the message can be reinforced (showing you care, or are concerned) by your presence, or in how you say it, using a messenger (e-mail) can destroy a relationship and build distrust.

For similar reasons, a leader "should command from well forward. This allows him to see and sense firsthand the ebb and flow, to gain an intuitive appreciation for the situation which he cannot obtain from reports. It allows him to exert his personal influence at decisive points." (63) "Only by his physical presence can the commander gain the trust and confidence." (64) Leadership by its very definition is about a relationship between the leader and the follower, but we must also "remember that command from the front does not equate to oversupervision." (64) There is a fine line between being present and interfering. At the higher levels of leadership, leaders understand the difference and can remain conceptual.

Our philosophy of command "requires competent leadership at all levels. A centralized system theoretically needs only one competent person . . . the sole authority. But a decentralized system requires leaders at all levels to demonstrate sound and timely judgment. As a result, initiative becomes an essential condition of competence among commanders." (65)

"For commanders to try to gain certainty as a basis for actions, maintain positive control of events at all times, or shape events to fit their plans is to deny the very nature" (64) of today's conflicted world. "We must therefore be prepared to cope—even better, to thrive—in an environment of chaos, uncertainty, constant change, and friction. In practical terms this means that we must not strive for certainty before we act for in doing so we will surrender the initiative and pass up opportunities. We must not try to maintain positive control over" others "since this will necessarily slow our tempo and inhibit initiative." (64)

In the second wave Industrial Revolution, managers attempted to maintain positive control in the way they delegated tasks to others. Much has been written about how to effectively and efficiently delegate a task. In a maneuver way of thinking, there "are two parts to a mission: the task to be accomplished and the reason, or intent. The task describes the action to be taken while the intent describes the desired results of the action. Of the two, the intent is predominant. While a situation may change, making the task obsolete, the intent is more permanent and continues to guide our actions." (71)

Marines call this commander's intent, and it is a key concept in remaining conceptual. Communicating intent is also critical to philosophy of command. In business, the focus too often is on the task. The intent may not be communicated, understood, or even known. In today's world where tasks are often very complex, many are acknowledging their difficulty in delegating effectively. The blame is often placed on inadequate communication. A specific task is difficult to describe. The person delegating a task knows what needs to be accomplished, but lacks the ability to convey detailed instructions.

In some cases, if the instructions were followed exactly, the end result could be a disaster. In the extreme, people may complete the task they are told, knowing that it will produce a result that is the opposite of what was expected (intent). Some call this "malicious obedience." In today's world of rapid change, the overall objective can often change before the task is completed. As a result, there is the potential for wasting resources if efforts are continued. When the intent is known and understood, the task itself becomes less important and can be changed during execution.

Knowing intent is therefore a prerequisite for today's decentralized execution. It is the umbrella over our actions. "Understanding our commander's (leader's) intent allows us to exercise initiative in harmony with the (leader's) desires." (71) Simply stating that the intent is to accomplish the goal (win the battle or increase sales) is inadequate. To be fully understood, the leader must convey the intent (the why) along with the what, where, when, and who will be there to assist. Marine leaders do not state how, leaving that up to individual initiative. In addition, the intent must reflect the fluidity of the situation, identifying how a task flows from a prior result and shapes a following action.

The burden of understanding the intent falls on both the leader and the followers. The leader "must make perfectly clear the results he expects, but in such a way that does not inhibit initiative." (72) The followers "must have a clear understanding of what their commander is thinking." (72) A key belief is that the intent should be known and understood two levels up and two levels down. As noted above in our discussion of implicit communication, it is difficult to convey intent by using memos or technology (e-mail and voice mail). It requires personal, oral, and face-to-face communication. Frequently, it requires long answers to what might seem to be simple questions. The results will be worth the extra effort. Knowing and communicating the intent expands your ability to increase momentum, exploit opportunities, reduce self-induced friction, create unity, and build trust and familiarity.

> "Coordination of action is possible because the commander has expressed his intent and there exists a trust between the commander and the troops that the troops will act and make decisions in consonance with the commander's intent. Some erroneously label this as centralized planning, decentralized execution. What we are describing is centralized vision and decentralized decision making."
>
> Michael Myatt, Major General, USMC (Ret.)

Our next concept—decision making—"is essential since all actions are the result of decisions—or of nondecisions." (68) Of all the concepts we have presented, you may feel the most familiarity with decision making. But it is worth a new look in the light of the other maneuver concepts we have discussed. Remember the OODA loop? "Whoever can make and implement his decision consistently faster gains a tremendous, often decisive advantage. Decision making thus becomes a time-competitive process, and timeliness of decisions becomes essential to generating tempo." (69)

In business, as well as in the military, an individual's willingness to make a decision may be tied to courage and fear. And "courage is not the absence of fear; rather, it is the strength to overcome fear. Leadership must foster the courage to overcome fear, both individually and within the unit." (12) "If we fail to make a decision out of lack of will, we have willingly surrendered the initiative. If we consciously postpone taking action for some reason, that is a decision. Thus, as a basis for action, any decision is generally better than no decision." (68)

Remaining conceptual in conflict is more than a willingness to make a decision. It requires a foundation, what we have called a philosophy (defined as a system of ideas and a sum of ideals—personal convictions), upon which your decisions should be made. Although we will discuss values and culture in Chapter 10 as part of having commitment, we cannot, and should not, prescribe your personal leadership philosophy. Like *Warfighting* itself, we can only provide you "broad guidance in the form of concepts and values . . . a philosophy for action . . . a way of thinking in general." (Foreword) What follows then can only be broad guidance on decision making. Because it is directly applicable, it is presented with little additional comments. It will require judgment, your judgment, in applying. We will provide you additional guidance on exercising judgment at the end of the chapter.

"Timely decisions demand rapid thinking, with consideration limited to essential factors. We should spare no effort to accelerate our decision-making ability." (69) But a decision "is not merely a mathematical computation. Decision making requires both the intuitive skill to recognize and analyze the essence of a given problem and the creative ability to devise a practical solution. This ability is the product of experience, education, intelligence, boldness, perception, and character." (69)

"We should base our decisions on *awareness* rather than on mechanical *habit*. That is, we act on a keen appreciation for the essential factors that make each situation unique instead of from a conditioned response. We must have the moral courage to make tough decisions in the face of uncertainty—and to accept full responsibility for those decisions—when the natural inclination would be to postpone the decision pending more complete information. We do not want to make rash decisions, but we must not squander opportunities while trying to gain more information." (69)

"Finally, since all decisions must be made in the face of uncertainty and since every situation is unique, there is no perfect solution to any . . . problem. Therefore, we should not agonize over one. The essence of the problem is to select a promising course of action with an acceptable degree of risk, and to do it more quickly than our" (70) competition. Simply put, the best decision is a decision. Searching for the perfect decision too often results in no decision or a decision made too late to be effective.

Now that we have discussed philosophy of command, commander's intent, and decision making as part of an overall (conceptual) way of thinking, we can now (as promised above) turn our attention to the exercise of judgment. Some may say that decision making and judgment are the same concept. We believe they are similar, but exercising judgment goes beyond just making a decision.

Judgment is one of those terms that everyone seems to feel they understand, but few ever attempt to define in their own terms. We did in Chapter 4, in our discussion of the Judgment Revolution—"Our use of judgment to describe the fourth wave is based on the definitions tied to the ability to make well-reasoned choices from existing and possible opportunities. Our exercise of judgment is based on experiences and values. It is an ability shared by many (and able to be developed by many more), not a trait possessed by a relatively few."

To test both our definition and our belief, we asked people what judgment and exercising judgment means to them. We found the results to be both interesting and informative.

> "Judgment is applying a lifetime of experiences within a framework of values."
>
> Bob Bailey, retired Chairman and CEO,
> State Auto Insurance Companies

> "We exercise judgment based on three things—past experiences, our conceptual compass, and intuition. Exercising judg-

ment becomes more difficult when we are in 'uncharted waters' or a state of uncertainty."

Jane Robinson, Chief Talent Officer
Franklin University

"Judgment to me is dealing in uncertainty. Judgment is the intuitive thinking that takes over when analytical methods have reached an end. It is not based on logic. It is based on experience and acquired knowledge."

Ron Hartung, Chair Computer Science,
Franklin University

"Consistently good judgment is an essential component of leadership built on intelligence, charisma, and strength of character. It results in making the best choice from competing courses of action in something major like moving an organization in a non-traditional direction, or something (relatively) minor like correcting institutional predispositions."

Scott Laidig, Vice President, VisiCom
Laboratories, Inc. Former Captain, USMC

"Judgment is the thoughtful weighing of alternatives, leading to a confident and courageous expression or action, for which the leader accepts the consequences or outcomes."

Marsha Ryan, President and COO
Indiana Michigan Power Company (AEP)

"Judgment is demonstrated in the personal actions and decisions of an individual that are tempered and influenced by experience, maturity, and morality. It is specific when it occurs; it happens at a particular time. A person's judgment can be significantly altered from predictable paths if circumstances dictate."

Cliff Stanley, Major General, USMC (Ret.) and
President Scholarship America

There are common elements in each of the above statements. All are good descriptions of our world today and reinforce our belief that we have entered the fourth wave, Judgment Revolution. Some are more complex than others. In the most simplistic form, they are all saying judgment is doing the right thing *always.* A simple statement, but like the concept of boldness (discussed above) it frequently may be the most difficult path to take.

Which definition of judgment is the most meaningful to you? The answer, of course, is yours. As a Conflicted Leader, in today's Judgment Revolution, we encourage you to consider (and even write) what judgment and exercising judgment means to you. You might also find it helpful (and interesting) to ask people whose opinions you value for theirs. In the long term, your success will be dependent on exercising your judgment. But for now, we have established a solid enough footing to move to the next chapter and continue our discussion of remaining conceptual in conflict.

Vantage Leadership				
Chapter	Higher Levels of Leadership Themes		Concepts *(from Warfighting)*	Applied
5	Seeing the Possible over the Probable		*attrition thinking* *maneuver thought process*	being opportunistic
6	Staying Focused Despite Uncertainty	building momentum	*concentration* *speed (velocity and tempo)* *surprise* *boldness*	organizing for momentum
7	Staying Focused Despite Uncertainty	without creating certainty	*friction* *uncertainty* *fluidity* *disorder*	exploiting opportunities
8	Remaining Conceptual	in conflict	*Philosophy of command (implicit communications)* *commander's intent* *decision making*	judgment
9	Remaining Conceptual	end state planning	*focus of effort* *shaping the situation (spheres of interest and influence)* *mission tactics*	campaign planning (exercises, critiques)
10	Having Commitment and a Sense of Presence	courage/resolve passion values/culture		professional education
10	Having Commitment and a Sense of Presence	in time and place selflessness		all or none?

CHAPTER NINE

Vantage Leadership—Remaining Conceptual—End State Planning

The concept of knowing where you are going is far from new. Most will remember the scene from Lewis Carroll's 1865 classic *Alice's Adventures in Wonderland*, when Alice asks Cheshire Puss, "Would you tell me, please, which way I ought to go from here? That depends a good deal on where you want to get to, said the Cat. I don't much care where—said Alice. Then it doesn't matter which way you go, said the Cat.—so long as I get somewhere, Alice added as an explanation. Oh, you're sure to do that, said the Cat, if you only walk long enough."

More recently, Stephen Covey in his 1990 best seller, *The 7 Habits of Highly Effective People*, advised us to "begin with the end in mind."[17] Our definition of leadership in the Prologue, "leadership is the relationship between a leader and a follower in the achievement of a positive goal" and the definition in our Chapter 5 from FMFM 1–1 *Campaigning*, "Leadership is the personal ability to influence the performance of human beings in pursuit of a goal," are both consistent with the concept of beginning with the end in mind, knowing where you are going, and what the Marine's call, the end state.

Not surprisingly, in response to our nation's call—"Send in the Marines"—Marine leaders ask, "What do you want it to look like, when we are finished?" This concept of end state planning is a key to understanding our higher level of leadership theme, remaining conceptual in conflict. It is supported by our discussion of the philosophy of command, commander's intent, and decision making in the last chapter and accomplished through the concepts of focus of effort, shaping the situation, and mission tactics discussed below.

To many, this end state way of thinking is antithetical to their way of proceeding. They prefer to begin with the current state and project it forward. For them, change is best addressed through an evolutionary process. But today's leader is in an environment filled with chaos, uncertainty, and conflict. Faced with multiple revolutions all impacting at the same time, the Conflicted Leader needs a revolutionary way of thinking that begins with the end state and builds a bridge back to today, a bridge that focuses not on what is probable, but on what is possible.

Building a bridge backward is a leader's way of creating a path that others can follow as they are led through the uncertainty. It is a new way of creating and communicating a "vision" of a higher level of success, because the leader who follows end state thinking looks farther out than others. This is the key to remaining conceptual in conflict. The farther out you look, the more conceptual your view must become. And the more rapid the change, the farther ahead you have to look to be prepared for today. The old advice of "keep your eye on the ball," should become for leaders "keep your focus on the future."

Having an end state and a conceptual way of thinking does not, in itself, guarantee your success in today's turbulent world. You must also learn to focus your efforts (a way of concentrating your resources), shape the situation (to gain the advantage), and lead through mission tactics (the intermediate steps along the way). We will explore each of these concepts in detail individually and then in total in our discussion of campaign planning (our end state for this chapter). Let's begin with understanding and applying the focus of effort.

"We cannot take lightly the decision of where and when to focus our efforts. Since the focus of effort represents our bid for (success), we must direct it at the object which . . . holds the best opportunity for success." (73) Do you remember our discussion of the maneuver concept of concentration in Chapter 6? The focus of effort is where the leader will concentrate resources. In business, resources can be applied to new (internal and externally generated) opportunities, as well as the weaknesses of competitors (another form of an opportunity). The result is "breakthrough" thinking—seeking and responding to the greatest potential.

"It involves a physical and moral commitment, although not an irretrievable one." (73) Once the focus of effort is established, its execution is aided by speed, surprise, and boldness. "Normally, we designate the focus of effort by assigning one unit responsibility for accomplishing that effort. It becomes clear to all other units . . . that they must support that unit in its efforts." (73) To some, this may seem inconsistent with today's emphasis on a team approach in business. It isn't, but it may require a change in the way you view the "team."

In end state thinking, all resources are committed to achieving the goal. Each "unit" supports the total team. At any point in time, one unit becomes the focus of effort with other units in support. All are moving together, as a team, in the same direction with the same focus to guide their efforts. In this way, you build on the capabilities of each unit and the total team. What about your organization? Do you know the focus of effort, or do multiple departments (units) view themselves as the focus, competing for (not concentrating) available resources?

Even if you have an agreed upon a focus for your efforts, are your unit leaders willing to relinquish the focus when situations change? "Each (leader) should establish a focus of effort for each mission. As the situation changes, the (leader) may shift the focus of effort." (73) Consider birds in flight. Much has been written about their leadership. Birds take turns leading the flock. They take the lead as long as they are capable and then turn the position over to the next leader. This is a clear example of focus of effort. A simple business example would be shifting the focus of effort from sales to service when problems arise.

The end state provides a description of the goal that must be communicated and reinforced in everything the leader and the followers do until the end state is achieved. "Having done this, we can determine the steps necessary to achieve our intent. That is, we must shape the battle (situation) to our advantage in terms of both time and space. Similarly, we must try to see ourselves through the eyes (of others) in order to identify our own vulnerabilities." (66)

You may feel it is inconsistent in today's world to think of shaping an uncertain situation. But remember, staying focused despite uncertainty doesn't create certainty. Nor does shaping the situation imply controlling it. It simply means defining your end state and your intent. "The first requirement is to establish your intent; what you want to accomplish and how. Without a clearly identified intent, the necessary unity of effort is inconceivable." (66) At the same time, "we cannot expect to shape its terms with any sort of precision. We must not become slaves to a plan. Rather, we attempt to shape the general conditions . . . we try to achieve a certain measure of ordered disorder." (67)

"The further ahead we think, the less our actual influence becomes. Therefore, the further ahead we consider, the less precision we should attempt to impose. Looking ahead thus becomes less a matter of influence and more a matter of interest. As events approach and our ability to influence them grows, we have already developed an appreciation for the situation and how we want to shape it." (67) In today's conflicted world, the idea of spheres of interest and influence are two ideas worth pursuing in greater depth.

Your sphere of interest represents those things that appeal to you, concern you, or even are just part of what you think about. Your sphere of influence includes the things you are capable of affecting. As might be expected, the things you are interested in would be much broader than those you can influence, and the more you are interested in something, the more likely you are to learn more about it. In periods of great uncertainty, change comes at you rapidly. The further out your sphere of interest, the more you have learned about things in advance, the better you will be able to react to change once it reaches your sphere of influence. From our observation, those who function at the higher levels of leadership have a broader sphere of interest than others in similar level positions.

In addition, the higher your position, "the greater is your sphere of influence and the further ahead in time and space you must seek to impose your will." (67) Think of the two spheres as concentric rings. As your sphere of influence increases along with your responsibilities, there is less time available to react to change that enters your sphere of interest. Broadening your interests will make you more aware and sooner, and as a result, you will be better prepared to succeed in today's chaotic, uncertain, and rapidly changing world. Sound too complex? It is an idea worth your greater understanding and interest.

Once you have your end state, your intent, have focused your efforts, and have shaped the situation, the next step is to put the maneuver way of thinking into practice "through the use of mission tactics. Mission tactics are just as the name implies: the tactic of assigning a mission without specifying how the mission must be accomplished. We leave the manner of accomplishing the mission to the subordinate, thereby allowing him the freedom—and establishing the duty—to take whatever steps he deems necessary based on the situation." (70) In others words, as stated above, Marines leave the how of mission tactics up to the individual.

Mission tactics support the maneuver thought process, and are supported by it in multiple ways. The leader "prescribes the method of execution only to the degree that is essential for coordination. (70–71) It is this freedom for initiative that permits the high tempo of operations that we desire." (71) And speed in one situation can provide an advantage in subsequent actions (fluidity). "Uninhibited by restrictions from above, the subordinate can adapt his actions to the changing situation." (71) A timely response can create surprise. In any situation with rapidly changing circumstances, there is often disorder and uncertainty.

By following mission tactics "he informs his (leader) what he has done, but does not wait for permission."(71) Each time an individual exercises judgment, initiative, and innovation, it adds greatly to future boldness. The same freedom that supports initiative also establishes the duty and the acceptance of responsibility for completing the mission through decentralized execution. This results in what Marines call a "force multiplier."

"It is obvious that we cannot allow decentralized initiative without some means of providing unity, or focus, to the various efforts. We seek unity, not through imposed control, but through harmonious initiative and lateral coordination." (71) Your focus of effort provides lateral coordination. Harmonious initiative is achieved through commander's intent. Mission tactics support decentralized decision making and are frequently carried out through quick actions and rote responses.

The advantage of mission tactics, shaping the situation, and focus of effort is best seen in how the Marines approach planning, in general, and in particular what they call campaign planning. In our view, there is a significant difference between planning in the Marines and in a typical business. Marines begin with an understanding that plans are based on assumptions and, as a result, they develop their plans considering the impact of many alternatives and they build in contingencies. Frequently, alternative plans are developed for each assumption.

Plans are not only kept simple, they also are extremely flexible. Leaders focus on the possible. Plans have broad parameters, fostering initiative and improvising as they are put into action. There is a willingness to accept, almost an expectation, that most plans will require quick and frequent modifications. Plans are seen more as a chess game. Each move is based on assumptions, but in each succeeding move, the assumptions change based on the last action of the opponent (remember Boyd's OODA Loop).

> "We have learned, to our regret, that while you are certainly better for preparing, the war you prepare for is rarely the war you get."
>
> Lt. General Victor "Brute" Krulak, USMC[18]

In businesses that focus on the probable, assumptions and contingencies may also be discussed, but with a desire for certainty, a single path may be selected early in the process. Alternatives, once dismissed as not probable, are often ignored in executing the plan. The plan itself is often elaborate, almost as if detail can create certainty. Once underway, there is little flexibility. Following our analogy, these business plans are more of a one-sided chess game. Each move follows a preconceived plan without considering the results in between.

The most successful businesses are the ones that take risks and can think beyond the probable to the possible. In today's futures-based scenario planning, the low probability items with high-impact potential, called "wild cards," are becoming more important. Trend watchers, who in the past would look for multiple occurrences, now think in terms of trends beginning with just one event, supported by others factors. As a result, leaders are frequently reacting like futurists—with less certainty and speeding up their reaction to events.

To exploit opportunities requires a plan for the long-term (a campaign), not a short-term plan that becomes outdated before it is finalized, or one that sits on a shelf, known to only a relative few. With a definable end state, campaign planning builds the bridge back to today broken down into logical, executable phases. Each phase is driven by the resources available (products, processes, and technology are examples) and implemented through a focus of effort. Phases may occur sequentially, simultaneously, or most likely a combination of both.*

"Each phase may be a single operation, or in the case of large campaigns, a minor campaign in itself. While each phase may be generally distinguishable from the others as a distinct episode, it is necessarily linked to the others and gains significance only in the larger context of the campaign." (44C) "Each phase of the campaign is generally aimed at some intermediate goal necessary to the ultimate accomplishment of the larger aim of the campaign. While we may envision each phase lasting a certain duration, the phases of a campaign are event-oriented rather than time-oriented." (45C)

"The further ahead we project, the less certain and detailed will be our design. We may plan the initial phase of a campaign with some degree of certainty, but since the results of that phase will shape the phases that follow, subsequent plans will become increasingly general. The design for future phases may consist of no more than contin-

---

***Note**: The concept of a campaign, both its design (planning) and conduct, is presented in detail in FMFM 1–1 *Campaigning* (a companion book to *Warfighting*, published by the Marine Corps in 1990). Consistent with our approach, in our discussion of campaign planning below, the numbers in parenthesis after the quotes are the pages numbers from *Campaigning*.

gencies, options, and a general intent." (45C) In long range planning, the campaign may set goals twenty years into the future. Phases would include objectives spread over the mid-range years. Tactics should focus on building capabilities for the year after next.

"But at the same time, we cannot devise any sequence of events without . . . the desired end state clearly in mind—even while recognizing its tentative nature—from which we envision a reasonable series of phases backward toward the present." (46C) "The campaign plan establishes tentative milestones and becomes a measure of progress, but is not a schedule in any final immutable sense. Until the final aim is realized, we must continuously adapt our campaign plan to changing aims, results, resources, and limiting factors." (51C) It is this flexibility in thinking that separates campaign planning from most business plans. As stated initially, the expectation that plans will change as the situation develops leads to a campaign that is more flexible, adjusts to changing assumptions, new alternatives, and the impact of contingencies.

"The campaign plan should be concise. The campaign plan does not describe the execution of its phases in tactical detail. Rather it provides guidance for developing the operational plans, which will in turn provide the tactical design for those phases." (51C) Like maneuver thinking, campaign planning requires judgment in application. The more complex, lengthy, and detailed a plan is, the less likely it can be implemented.

"While the tactician looks at the immediate tactical problem and the conditions directly preceding and following, the (leader) must take a broader view. He must not become so involved in tactical activities that he loses his proper perspective. This broader perspective implies broader dimensions of time and space over which to apply the art. The (leader) must use all the time and space within his influence to create the conditions for success." (62C) Keeping your perspective is the desired end state for those who function at the higher levels of leadership. They learn to balance the attention to details without losing sight of the broader view. The learned leader knows that the higher up one goes in an organization, success must be judged over a longer period. The idea of the leader's perspective in time and space will be considered in greater detail as part of our discussion of a sense of presence in the next chapter.

Before moving to the next chapter, however, there are two techniques used by Marines in campaign planning that could greatly benefit leaders in any organization: they are exercises and critiques. To think through their plans and the consequences of each action, Marines use exercises. As a planning tool, these exercises develop scenarios, evaluating the strengths and weaknesses of each alternative. They then identify different courses of actions for each set of circumstances and develop options that can be employed quickly if the situation changes. Compare this approach to guiding a boat down a river. On a nautical map, each island would be identified in advance. When reaching a fork in the river, the benefits and disadvantages of each path would have been discussed in advance and a tentative decision made, subject to updating as needed. This is the essence of an exercise.

Many in business might respond negatively to the suggestion of exercises and be quick to point out there is little time to practice before execution in today's chaotic world. We would propose that the lack of considering the consequences of actions, the failure to explore alternatives and adequately evaluate assumptions, and the reluctance to develop options, along with the unwillingness to change directions once a plan or idea is put in place, has led to the loss of great amounts of time (as well as money) as organizations are forced to dig themselves out from the results of plans blindly followed. Exercises in business need not be as elaborate as the large scale maneuvers employed in the military. They could be as simple as an honest and open discussion in the conference room. This leads us to the next technique, critiques.

Marines consider critiques as an important part of leadership development. Critiques are conducted immediately after events, even those that are successful. They are seen as an opportunity to learn. "Critiques should be held in atmosphere of open and frank dialogue in which all hands are encouraged to contribute. We learn as much from mistakes as from things done well, so we must be willing to admit and discuss them." (49)[19] Marines are encouraged to "leave their rank on the table," as critiques are intended to draw out criticism from all participants.

Of course, an individual's willingness to identify or admit their own mistakes is dependent on others "willingness to tolerate them." (49) You might say people in your organization lack the courage for open and frank dialogue. This might be more of a reflection of the leader's behaviors than the followers. A key is to "focus not so much on the actions we took as on why we took those actions and why they brought the results they did." (49) Critiques should consider the focus of effort, mission tactics, decisions made, and whether the end state was clearly communicated through commander's intent.

"Critiques should be lenient and understanding, rather than bitter and harsh. Mistakes are essential to the learning process and should be cast in a positive light. The focus should not be on whether the leader did well or poorly, but on what progress he is making in his overall development as a leader. We must aim to provide the best climate to grow leaders."[20]

Remember, our goal is to grow leaders who can function at the higher levels of leadership—seeing the possible over the probable, staying focused despite uncertainty, remaining conceptual in conflict, and having commitment. We are now ready to begin our discussion of commitment in the next chapter.

Vantage Leadership				
Chapter	Higher Levels of Leadership Themes		Concepts *(from Warfighting)*	Applied
5	Seeing the Possible over the Probable		*attrition thinking* *maneuver thought process*	being opportunistic
6	Staying Focused Despite Uncertainty	building momentum	*concentration* *speed (velocity and tempo)* *surprise* *boldness*	organizing for momentum
7		without creating certainty	*friction* *uncertainty* *fluidity* *disorder*	exploiting opportunities
8	Remaining Conceptual	in conflict	*Philosophy of command (implicit communications)* *commander's intent* *decision making*	judgment
9		end state planning	*focus of effort* *shaping the situation (spheres of interest and influence)* *mission tactics*	campaign planning (exercises, critiques)
10	Having Commitment and a Sense of Presence	courage/ resolve passion values/culture		professional education
		in time and place selflessness		all or none?

CHAPTER TEN

Vantage Leadership—Having Commitment and a Sense of Presence

Let's summarize our progress so far. We began by presenting the waves of change and the resulting revolutions. In doing so, we made what we believe is a strong case in support of today's Conflicted Leader. In response to the conflict, uncertainty, and chaos that are part of the revolutions, we introduced a new model of leadership that merges the higher level of leadership themes, first proposed in the Introduction, with the concepts embedded in the maneuver way of thinking as documented in *Warfighting*.

At this point, it would be helpful to return to our Vantage Leadership chart, first presented in A Second Prologue, to show how far we have come on our journey. We have discussed seeing the possible over the probable (Chapter 5), staying focused despite uncertainty (Chapters 6 and 7), and remaining conceptual in conflict (Chapters 8 and 9). Along the way, we have introduced and applied more than two dozen concepts that are critical components in the maneuver thought process.

For Marines, this philosophy represents their doctrine. For you, its broad guidance, concepts, and values provide the foundation for Vantage Leadership and, as we have shown, can easily be applied to leadership in any organization. Until now, our discussion has focused more on the Marines' way of thinking and their concepts, and less on their values. But it is their strong values and culture that will provide us the best examples of having commitment and a sense of presence—our next higher level of leadership themes.

Once again, we should emphasize our intent is not to recruit you into the Marines. We assume the greatest majority of our readers are either too old or too established in their careers to make such a major lifestyle change. But we also assume, since you have stayed with us this far, that you want to be a better leader and are willing to continue your journey on the path to Vantage Leadership and our next theme, having commitment.

Although there are similarities in the dictionary between definitions of committed and commitment, we think there are also differences. Many, if not most, people are committed to something. It could be a belief, a cause, or even a sports team. Commitment, in our opinion, goes further. It requires courage, passion, and the resolve to see things to their end state. Think of how the most committed fans may abandon their teams in a losing season.

For a leader, commitment goes hand-in-hand with duty and responsibility. It often requires courage in face of uncertainty and conflict (real or imagined). In many (business, government, community, or educational) organizations there seem to be an abundance of people who know what needs to be done, but fewer who have the courage to do it. Commitment includes not only having beliefs and values, but living by them, and leading others with and through the same beliefs and values, most frequently by setting the example. It is, as stated before, doing the right thing, always.

Unlike the themes and the many concepts we have already discussed, your commitment is closely tied to the organization you serve. You can develop and demonstrate your ability to see the possible, stay focused, and remain conceptual in most, if not all, settings. But your commitment is closely linked to your values and beliefs, as well as your organization's. It is hard for us to imagine someone having a lasting commitment in an institution whose values conflict with their own. It makes us wonder about turnover in today's business world. How much attrition can be attributed to incompatible values, in both directions?

Likewise, the lack of commitment and the conflict in values may be the reason why many mergers and acquisitions fail to integrate the companies' respective cultures. What may look good on paper, the bringing together of the resources of two organizations, cannot ignore that each organization has its own culture, values, and way of doing things. And, as noted above, people build a commitment to organizations based on shared values. Any merger creates great uncertainty as people are brought together and a new culture is formed. When values clash, commitments can be broken.

Like leaders, organizations themselves can demonstrate their commitment. Some might be quick to point out that a public corporation's commitment is to the stockholders. We believe any successful organization must have commitment beyond just those who own stock. It might surprise you, but even corporate law provides that a board member "may consider the interests of its other constituencies, including; interests of the employees, suppliers, creditors, and customers; the local, state, and national economy; and community and societal considerations."[21]

At the higher levels of leadership, leaders know their greatest commitment must be to the people they lead. These leaders care more about their people than themselves and it is evident in everything they do (not just what they say). Because they care about the people they have responsibility for, they are never too busy to listen to them. Listening builds both trust and commitment.

You can also find commitment by listening to your leaders. No matter how introverted a leader with commitment might be, they speak with a passion when they are describing their intent, their end state, or their people. They talk in terms of "we" when referring to their organization and their people and use "I" sparingly, except when mistakes are made (they take personal responsibility). Leaders who lack commitment to their people and their organizations seem to say "they" more often, especially when a mistake is made and responsibility is being avoided.

Leaders with commitment have a passion that is contagious, and as a result these are the leaders who people want to follow. How many leaders have commitment? Look at your own organization. How many of your leaders are committed? The answer may be found in which ones you want to (not just are willing to) follow and why.

Some leaders may profess a loyalty to their people and their organizations. They may speak with a passion, but down deep their passion and their loyalty is to themselves and their careers. Leaders who lack commitment seem to be able to work in any organization and they seek assignments that provide any opportunity to advance their own careers. As a result, they may be the first to leave when problems arise because they do not want it on their resume.

Unfortunately, the lack of commitment sometimes becomes clear only when a leader leaves an organization (or unit). They just move on, without looking back, sometimes looking to their next promotion even before they have begun their new position. This doesn't mean that those with commitment never leave. They are often promoted, or recruited away. But their commitment stays with them, it is infinite. Have you ever heard "once a Marine, always a Marine?" Marines are quick to point out there are no "ex-Marines," only current or former Marines.

Whenever possible, leaders who have commitment are quick to offer support to the people who made them successful or to the organization that provided them the opportunity. What about the leader who had the commitment but seems to have lost it over time? There can be several reasons for the loss. Sometimes just having to work for a leader who lacks commitment can reduce your own. In other situations, an individual with commitment can be promoted to a leader's position but not be given (or not seek out) leadership development opportunities. In today's conflicted times, continuous learning is fundamental to any individual's development and without it a leader can be overtaken by events. In these cases, like the child who stops drawing, the result is a leader who stops (or never starts) leading.

The long-term solution is to go beyond courage and build the resolve needed to lead in today's conflicted times. Conflict, of any type, tests commitment. And in the Marines, we have the ultimate conflict-tested organization. You can see it in their values and their culture, an ethos. It begins with their core values: honor (integrity, responsibility, accountability), courage (doing the right thing, in the right way, for the right reasons), and commitment (devotion to the Corps and fellow Marines).[22]

You may be quick to point out that many organizations have values, but a difference may be in how the Marine Corps inculcates their values and builds commitment through their professional education. Their educational programs go well beyond enlisted boot camp and officer training; most important is their end state, "to develop creative, thinking leaders." (49) A leader in the Corps is either learning, doing, or teaching. "A leader's career, from the initial stages of leadership training, should be viewed as a continuous, progressive process of development. At each stage of his career, he should be preparing for the next stage." (49)

While many may talk in support of lifelong learning, the Marines practice it every day, at all levels. "The responsibility for implementing . . . education in the Marine Corps is three tiered: it resides not only with the education establishment, but also with the commander (leader) and the individual." (50) Consistent with their maneuver thought process, their education focuses "on developing a talent for judgment, not imparting knowledge through rote learning." (50–51)

Every Marine leader is expected to know themselves, their people, and their profession. All leaders "should consider the professional development of their (people) a principal responsibility." (51) Leaders "should foster a personal teacher-student relationship. A leader without either interest in or knowledge of the history and theory—the intellectual content of his profession—is a leader in appearance only." (51) This is summed up in the statement, a leader's "principal weapon is his mind." (51)

There are many similarities in how other organizations and the Marines approach education, but there are also key differences in their focus of effort, intent, tactics, and end states. Too much of education, especially at the lower levels, but also in our universities with their large lecture halls, is still focused on "imparting knowledge through rote learning," not "to develop creative, thinking leaders," or "building a talent for judgment," even though we have entered the Judgment Revolution. Business leaders are taking a more active role in guiding their community's education programs, but many still fail to understand the "three-tiered" responsibility, linking the schools, their leadership, and the individual.

Many businesses are investing considerable resources in educating their workforce, but the focus remains more on today's assignments than preparing for the next stage. This is reflected in tuition reimbursement programs, which are most often seen as an employee benefit and not managed as an investment in the future, the organization's as well as the individual's. Consider the tremendous loss when individuals leave an organization that has just paid for their college education to seek greater opportunities elsewhere because their education has not built a commitment in either direction.

Do your leaders "see the development of their people as a direct reflection on themselves?" (51) Do you see the development of your people as your leadership legacy? Do you get "psychic income" from watching them grow? Is it reflected in your goals and in your organization's evaluation process? If not, you may not be building commitment, either yours or your people's.

You may have never thought about commitment being achieved through education, but it is through educational programs that organizations convey their values, develop courage and resolve, build passion, and show their commitment to people. We would go as far as to say—if you aren't teaching, you aren't leading.

Remember when we first proposed the four higher level of leadership themes? We said they applied to leaders regardless of their organizational level or position. After our verifying discussions with several leaders, it became apparent that there is a fifth theme that does relate to hierarchical level; it is a sense of presence. Like the other themes we have already presented, our definition of the term may differ from common interpretations. To many, a sense of presence relates to an individual's personal charisma, granting leaders an almost celebrity status. It shouldn't surprise you that our view is much broader, as it encompasses the dimensions of both time and space (as we noted in Chapter 9 in our discussion of perspective).

Remember also the quote from above, "A leader without either interest in or knowledge of the history and theory—the intellectual content of his profession—is a leader in appearance only." (51) Over time many successful leaders expand their sphere of interest to include the history of their organization, their industry, their community, and their nation (and the world). Those who understand history have a greater sense of their presence in time, and since as many have noted "history repeats itself," they are better prepared to lead when events unfold in their sphere of influence.

Like the maneuver concept of fluidity, our sense of presence reflects an individual's position in relation to who (and what) preceded the leader, as well as who (and what) will follow (the dimension of time). It also includes the impact a leader has on the organization, as well as all of the organization's internal and external influences on the leader (a dimension in space). You may think these are unnecessary, or overly simplistic, statements, but when you consider the number of times a new person assumes a leadership position and seems to forget the people who helped along the way, those who preceded the leader in the same position, or the many (current and former) people in the organization who made it what it already is, it is a necessary reminder.

Anyone who has attended the morning colors after the Crucible event at Marine Corps' boot camp and witnessed the awarding of the Marine Corps eagle, globe, and anchor has seen first hand the emotions associated with an individual taking his or her place in the history of a proud organization. The recruit, now Marine, is given an emblem that symbolizes becoming part of an institution that is older than our nation, being held accountable for continuing the traditions, and being responsible for its future. It is a simple ceremony with deep meaning, and it results in very few dry eyes in the crowd.

Of course, if you have ever seen Marines in their dress blue uniforms, either at a parade or formal ceremony at any location, you might notice that Marines have a great sense of presence—and they do, from the privates to the generals. But they would be quick to point out that it is the Marine Corps' sense of presence and it applies to all Marines. Through traditions, like privates eating first and generals last, they emphasize the importance of every Marine.

Some might suggest we add the descriptor "realistic" to our sense of presence, and we wouldn't disagree. Some leaders unfortunately seem to develop an over-inflated sense of their importance. Sure, a single leader can make a significant difference, but remember our definition of leadership is based on a relationship between a leader and followers and, as a result, no leader is entirely alone in accomplishing a goal. Like the maneuver concepts of speed, surprise, and boldness, a sense of presence should be judged relative to others. The further leaders separate themselves from the people in an organization, the less likely they will be to build their commitment.

How does a sense of presence relate to hierarchical levels? As noted above, we believe it is relative to other positions. At the Chief Executive Officer (CEO) position, a sense of presence is more often viewed from an external (charismatic) perspective. Surely, the CEO represents the organization in the local and even national community. The CEO also creates a sense of presence within the organization. At the Vice President's level, a leader's sense of presence is generally more internal (with colleagues) than external. And at levels below the VPs a sense of presence is created with one's peers in the organization.

At every level, a leader's presence is set in relationships with the people he or she serves. Leaders set standards for excellence, lead by example, and reinforce values through their physical presence at places and times that send a message of what and who are important. Those who are at the higher levels of leadership have a keen appreciation for the message their presence, or absence, sends.

Jo Ann Davidson, former Speaker of the Ohio House of Representatives, clearly leads through a sense of presence. She knew there were times when she should cast the first vote (leading by example), the last vote (supporting the leadership of others), or even choosing not to vote (a message in itself).

Lewis Smoot, Sr., CEO, following the guiding principles of Smoot Construction— character, humility, integrity, pride, performance and profitability ($CHIP^3$)—chose not to put the company's name on their new office building. This not only creates a sense of presence (by absence) but reinforces the humility of this leader and this nationally known firm.

Walk with a leader at the higher levels of leadership and watch how people seem to stand taller once they are close enough to recognize the leader and sense his or her presence. Bob Bailey, the retired CEO and Chairman of State Auto Insurance Companies and author of *Plain Talk About Leadership*,[23] would create a noticeable difference in the company cafeteria by his presence. Not because it was unusual for him to eat with the people of State Auto (he did it frequently) and not because of any celebrity status (Bob never lost his farmer-turned-insurance-salesman demeanor), but because of the respect he gave and received.

Some fail to recognize how a sense of privilege (reserved parking, executive dining rooms, and even separate executive elevators) can impact one's sense of presence, while others realize how they lead by their examples. We have seen leaders who just carry a particular book with them that quickly becomes "required" reading among others in the organization. When a professional reading program was created by General Gray, there was no need to issue an order for Marines at all ranks (from private to general) to read. They did, and continue to, because of the examples set by their leaders, including the Commandant.

Those who are seen as leaders have followers who are watching what they do, don't do, and (in the minds of others) should do. A sense of presence comes more from day-to-day encounters than ceremonial events. Those at the higher levels of leadership know the importance of just "stopping by" another's office or work area. They build relationships by keeping in mind what others are doing for them, or they are doing for the other individual, and then in quick follow-up conversations create both a sense of presence and fluidity.

Although a sense of presence relates to hierarchical level, it doesn't come by simply being promoted. The earlier we can identify individuals who demonstrate a sense of presence by the examples they set and their relationships with others, the sooner we can begin to build leadership talent at the higher levels. How can you recognize the potential? Look for those who are willing to place the needs of others ahead of their own.

Of all the concepts that support the higher levels of leadership, if we were required to pick only one—the one that does more to identify both the presence of, and the potential for, the higher levels of leadership; the one that underlies all of the themes—it would be the concept of selflessness. If having charisma is the external indicator of a sense of presence, being selfless is its internal equivalent. And of the two, selflessness is by far the most important.

No matter how much you develop your leadership, or how well you can see the possible, stay focused, remained conceptual, and have commitment and a sense of presence, unless you are willing to place your people ahead of yourself, you will never gain their total commitment. Selfish leaders can rarely be successful beyond the short-term.

In the long-term, people follow people that they trust, respect, and believe will lead them through the uncertainty and the conflict. Leadership is, as we have defined it, built on a relationship between a leader and a follower and relationships, as stated above, "should foster a personal teacher-student relationship." Successful teachers, like successful leaders, place the needs of their students ahead of their own.

Which leads us to the question—must a leader posses all the elements of the, now five, higher level of leadership themes to be successful? There is a definite synergism in the themes, and the absence of any one can reduce the effectiveness of the whole. Losing one's focus in uncertainty greatly reduces an individual's chance at achieving the end state. Remaining conceptual may best be answered not by a simple yes or no, but more by a level of conceptual thinking. As we stated above, the further out one can see the end state, the more conceptual they become. Likewise, seeing the possible over the probable is not an on-off switch. One leader cannot see all the possibilities, but this way of thinking can be nurtured in an organization so all leaders have a greater chance of seeing all possibilities. Just think of how large the sphere of interest could be in a thinking organization.

Unfortunately, the one theme that would seem most important—having commitment—is also the one that in our opinion is often missing; because leaders fail in their ability to develop it, but more likely they fail to find an organization in which they can build it. One where the values, beliefs, way of thinking, and desired end state, closely resemble their own. The closer you are to the top of an organization, the more likely you can change the culture, but it is a long, slow, sometimes uncertain, but often rewarding process. It takes courage and resolve.

A final question for now—Is the maneuver way of thinking the only way to develop the higher level of leadership themes? The concepts of maneuver are not the only way, but they are a well-traveled and well-documented (through *Warfighting*) path. Maneuver is a way of thinking that has served well both a great institution and a great nation. We offer it to you, not as the answer, but in the form of broad guidance. It will require your judgment in applying. It provides the foundation for a new model, Vantage Leadership. Its successful application depends on you, the Conflicted Leader.

The Final Prologue

Since we have already introduced a Second Prologue, some might not be surprised by the heading The Final Prologue. Others would expect we would finish with an Epilogue. We are concerned that an Epilogue implies an ending when your leadership journey may be just beginning. For us, The Final Prologue reflects a stopping point, a chance to summarize how far you have come and to state one more time the key concepts, ideas, and ideals we have presented. It also signals that most of your leadership journey lies ahead of you.

For many of you, your journey may have begun long before you began reading this book. For some, your search for a new leadership model may have led you to our book. For others, it may have been your knowledge of, and respect for, General Gray's leadership. While for others, it is required reading in your Vantage MBA program. But whenever you began, or whatever your reason, you have reached this (we believe, important) point on your journey.

Looking back, we began with an Introduction citing the reasons behind the book and introducing our teacher, General Gray. For those who might not have been ready for a new model of leadership, we first presented the waves of change and the resulting revolutions, all within the context of leadership. As a result, we hope, we made a strong case for describing today's leader as conflicted and the need for a new form of leadership. As promised, we presented a leadership model and a new way of thinking based on concepts found in a maneuver thought process as developed by General Gray and the United States Marine Corps.

We also introduced you to the higher level of leadership themes and demonstrated how the maneuver concepts not only supported but also further developed them. Along the way, we provided you with numerous examples of how the concepts and the themes can be applied in any organization. We encouraged you time and time again to look inward, at yourself and your organization, to question how and why you can develop your own leadership.

Surely, you have already seen and experienced (before and during your reading of this book) some, if not many, of the concepts we have described on your own leadership journey. Psychologists tell us that after being introduced to something, or making a decision (buying a car, for example), people will naturally observe it more often in their everyday activities. If so, you may now be seeing more frequently in your own organization the concepts and leadership themes we have presented. Or if they are missing, you may be more aware of their absence and the need for a new, higher level leadership approach.

As did *Warfighting*, we have presented the concepts, themes, and our leadership model in the form of guidance. Together they represent a way of thinking. It requires your judgment in its application. We have purposely kept the book short and (hopefully) easy to read. We encourage you to reread it, to share its contents with others. We have been told many times that those who reread *Warfighting* find new ideas, new applications, and reinforce their beliefs every time they read it, or even read parts of it. Our goal (end state) is for you to incorporate as much (or as little) of what we have presented into your thinking as you further develop your own leadership philosophy. What follows are the key ideas we hope you will consider.

We live in a world of chaos, change, and uncertainty. Change and uncertainty have been part of every period beginning with the nomadic era. In today's world, change is both rapid and sustained, which results in increased uncertainty. There is no expectation the future will move any slower (and there may be even more change).

Leaders who can exploit the opportunities this presents will thrive in a seemingly ever more chaotic world.

Along with employment and behavior factors shifting, the waves of change brought us the Agricultural, Industrial, Knowledge, and now, Judgment Revolutions. Over time, leadership has both been reflected in, and shaped by, the revolutions. No longer linear in their movement, the waves and the revolutions are now simultaneously impacting today's leaders. This has produced what we are calling the Conflicted Leader.

Leaders have been present from the beginning of time, leading people through uncertainty. Managers, a product of the Industrial Revolution, tried to create certainty through control, structure, and other management practices that are impacting us still today. To us, leadership is the natural state and management the exception, although it still dominates the minds of many.

What we need in our world of chaos, change, and uncertainty is a new model for leadership, one that can create superiority over conflict and break the lingering hold of "industrial" management. We call it Vantage Leadership and have presented it along with the higher level of leadership themes—seeing the possible over the probable, staying focused despite uncertainty, remaining conceptual in conflict, having commitment and a sense of presence.

Vantage Leadership is based on the concepts and the maneuver thought process found in *Warfighting*, a USMC publication, but it applies to leadership in any setting. The maneuver way of thinking is a clear example of seeing the possible over the probable. Leaders who can see the possible are being opportunistic, creating a decisive advantage in today's uncertain world.

Leaders lead through uncertainty, and leadership at the higher levels requires staying focused, without creating certainty. Through understanding and applying the concepts of concentration and speed, momentum can be built and sustained through the elements of surprise and boldness. The OODA loop (observation, orientation, decision, and action) provides us the best test of maintaining momentum.

Remember, managers attempt to create certainty, which often increases friction and works against momentum through increased controls and structure. The greatest damage occurs, however, through self-induced friction resulting from the lack of simple plans, unclear communications, and the failure to see and appreciate the fluidity and disorder in events.

Leadership at higher levels is directly related to the theme of remaining conceptual. The further ahead a leader can see the end state, the more conceptual he or she will become. In military conflict, Marines rely on their philosophy of command and commander's intent in their decision making. For today's Conflicted Leader, understanding and applying the concept of intent is critical to being conceptual. Intent is the umbrella over all actions. When intent is known two levels up and two levels down, you have an environment where people can demonstrate initiative, build momentum, and thrive (through letting go and watching people grow).

Remaining conceptual also means keeping your eyes on the end state. Simply put, it means asking and answering "What will it look like when it's finished?" Through the concept of campaign planning, a higher level of leadership is created by building a bridge from the end state back to the present. Then, through identifying a focus for your efforts, shaping the situation, and employing mission tactics effectively, you will be better able to accomplish your goal.

Although our intent is to provide guidance and not a recipe for leadership success, there are two techniques worth your consideration, exercises and critiques. In business, exercises need not be as extensive as military training. They can be an extension of planning that evaluates assumptions, considers alternatives, develops contingencies, and makes adjustments in execution based on periodic progress reviews.

Critiques should be performed for successes as well as failures. To be effective, participants should be encouraged to "take their rank off," allowing for open and honest discussion. People's willingness to admit their mistakes are tied to their leaders' tolerance to accept errors. Mistakes are both a great opportunity to demonstrate boldness in our actions to correct the problem and an opportunity for leadership development.

Having commitment is the one higher level of leadership theme that couples both the individual and the organization. It is hard to imagine a leader having commitment in an organization that does not share the same values and culture. Both of us have been fortunate. General Gray served 41 years in the Marine Corps, an institution with shared values, an ethos that bonds Marines to each other and the Corps. Paul Otte spent only four years in the Corps, enlisting at 17 years of age. But he has been with Franklin for almost 20 years and has seen its values (called guiding principles) well documented and applied across the university.

An individual's commitment is reflected in his or her character. To a leader it means having a commitment to your people. It requires having the ability to see what is needed and the courage to do it, the right thing, always. It is an unending courage, a resolve to not only see the end state, but to reach it, and lead others to it as well. Having commitment is communicated with a passion.

Values, culture, and passion can be shared and strengthened through your professional education programs. The sooner you can identify, nurture, educate, and promote people with the potential for the higher level of leadership themes, the stronger will be their commitment. To us, you lead others through teaching them.

A sense of presence is the only higher level of leadership theme that is directly related to the (hierarchical) position of an individual. The higher up one's position is, the more their presence is felt. Our sense of presence goes beyond charisma and focuses on the leader's position in the dimensions of both time and space. At the higher levels of leadership, the leader has a great understanding of the history surrounding their profession and the institution they serve. Knowing (and acknowledging) those who preceded you, along with a realization that others will occupy your position in the future brings a fluidity to your leadership.

Understanding your position in the dimension of space is equally important. Selfless leaders realize their greatest responsibility is to the people they are privileged to serve. Placing the needs of others ahead of oneself is a prerequisite to the highest levels of leadership.

Remember General Gray's early words of advice, "it will take you where it takes you." As we have reached a stopping point, it's time to ask, "How far have you traveled on your own leadership journey?" Looking backward from your desired end state—your own leadership philosophy—how much of what we have presented has been added to your bridge back to the present? No matter how much, or how little, you include, your journey is far from over. If you believe, like we do, that leadership is a natural state, your leadership development (learning, as well as teaching others) is a journey that never ends. Along the way, "Do as much good as you can, for as many people as you can, for as long as you can."[24]

Notes

1. This is a common phrase of General Gray's and the Marines.

2. Comments from the Foreword of FMFM 1 *Warfighting* are quoted at several points in this book. The entire Foreword follows:

DEPARTMENT OF THE NAVY
Headquarters United States Marine Corps
Washington, D. C. 20380-0001

6 March 1989

This book describes my philosophy on warfighting. It is the Marine Corps' doctrine and, as such, provides the authoritative basis for how we fight and how we prepare to fight.

By design, this is a small book and easy to read. It is not intended as a reference manual, but is designed to be read from cover to cover. There is a natural progression to its four chapters. Chapter 1 describes our understanding of the characteristics, problems, and demands of war. Chapter 2 derives a theory of war based on that understanding. This theory in turn provides the foundation for how we prepare for war and how we wage war, Chapters 3 and 4 respectively.

You will notice that this book does not contain specific techniques and procedures for conduct. Rather, it provides broad guidance in the form of concepts and values. It requires judgment in application.

I expect every officer to read—and reread—this book, understand it, and take its message to heart. The thoughts contained here represent not just guidance for actions in combat, but a way of thinking in general. This manual thus describes a philosophy for action which, in war and in peace, in the field and in the rear, dictates our approach to duty.

A. M. GRAY
General, U.S. Marine Corps
Commandant of the Marine Corps

3. Toffler, Alvin and Heidi *War and Anti-War* (New York: Warner Books, Inc., 1993), pg. 35.

4. Merriam-Webster Online Dictionary www.m-w.com.

5. Check dictionaries for vantage

6. Harris, Robert A. *The Plagiarism Handbook: Strategies for Preventing, Detecting, and Dealing with Plagiarism.* (Los Angeles: Pyrczak, 2001).

7. Keith Sward, *The Legend of Henry Ford* (New York: Rinehart, 1948) p. 32 cited by John Diebold in *Making the Future Work* (New York: Simon and Schuster, 1984), p. 211.

8. Drucker, Peter, F. "The Age of Social Transformation," *The Atlantic Monthly*, November 1994, p. 62.

9. *The Economist*, February 7, 1998, p. 63.

10. Toffler, Alvin and Heidi *War and Anti-War* (New York: Warner Books, Inc, 1993), pg. 66.

11. Thanks to Bob Olmstead at R. C. Olmstead for this insight.

12. FMFM 1–1 *Campaigning* (a companion piece to *Warfighting*) published by the U. S. Marine Corps, 25 January 1990.

13. You can find out more about Edward DeBono and his concept of vertical and lateral thinking on his website http://www.edwdebono.com and Tony Buzan's mind mapping at http://www.buzan.org.

14. General Gray and Colonel Boyd were long time colleagues and friends. They spent many hours together discussing the maneuver way of thinking. In the early 1980s General Gray invited Colonel Boyd to make presentations to the officers and NCOs (non-commissioned officers) of the 2nd Marine Expeditionary Force (II MEF).

15. From a private conversation with the author about his books *Leading Change* and *The Heart of Change,* Sept. 2005.

16. Clausewitz, *On War*, p. 121, cited in *Warfighting* p. 4.

17. Covey, Stephen R., *The 7 Habits of Highly Effective People* (New York: Simon and Schuster, 1989).

18. Krulak, Victor H. Lt. Gen. USMC (Ret.), *First to Fight* (New York: Simon and Schuster, 1984 and 1991), p. 200.

19. Page references have now returned to *Warfighting.*

20. Pages 100-101 in *Tactics,* FMFM 1–3 (a companion piece to *Warfighting*) published by the U. S. Marine Corps, 1 June 1991.

21. Ohio Revised Code (O. R. C.) 1702.30 (E).

22. From a USMC identification card.

23. Published by the Franklin University Press, 1993.

24. Advice frequently given by General Gray at the end of any speech, or presentation.

About the Authors

General Alfred M. Gray, USMC (Ret.)

In 1991, General Al Gray retired from the United States Marine Corps after 41 years of service. He enlisted in the Marine Corps in 1950 and was commissioned a Second Lieutenant in 1952 from the rank of Sergeant. General Gray has extensive command experience with infantry, artillery, special intelligence and special operations units as well as every type of Marine Air-Ground Task Force. From 1987 to 1991, General Gray served as a member of the Joint Chiefs of Staff and was the 29th Commandant of the Marine Corps. In this capacity, he served as a military advisor to the President. He institutionalized and published a warfighting philosophy for Marines and implemented a new long range strategic planning process for the Corps.

General Gray is currently the Chairman of the Board for GlobeSecNine, Inc., and Chairman of Potomac Institute for Policy Studies Board of Regents. He is a former Chairman of both California Microwave, Inc., and Columbia Research Corporation and serves on several corporate boards.

General Gray is currently the Chancellor of the Marine Military Academy, Chairman of the U.S. Marine Youth Foundation and Chairman of the Injured Marine Semper Fi Fund. He also serves as a trustee for Norwich University and the American Military University where he is Chairman Emeritus. He holds Honorary Doctorate degrees from Lafayette College, Monmouth University, Norwich University and the Defense Intelligence University.

Dr. Paul J. Otte

In 1986, Paul Otte began serving as President of Franklin University, the largest independent institution of higher learning in central Ohio, serving nearly 10,000 students annually.

Franklin University is known nationally for its relationship management approach to serving working adults through applied majors at the undergraduate level, as well as three graduate degrees, including the Vantage MBA. Founded over a hundred years ago with a mission of serving nontraditional students, today's Franklin has a strong culture, quality curriculum developed under an innovative academic model, expanded delivery options that include a Virtual Campus and a national and global presence through its Community College Alliance and eArmy U programs.

Dr. Otte also serves as Executive Director of Franklin's Leadership Center which was created in 2004 to serve as a resource for leadership development in business, government, community, and educational institutions.

Prior to joining Franklin, Dr. Otte was Vice President for Business at Macomb Community College in Warren, Michigan. He has taught at Wayne State University, the University of Detroit, Macomb Community College, and Franklin University. Formerly program chair for Franklin's undergraduate Organizational Leadership major, he currently serves as a professor in the program. He once worked as a CPA, but now considers himself "a recovering accountant." He enlisted in the Marine Corps when he was seventeen, served four years, achieved the rank of Corporal, and now realizes how much the experience changed him and provided the foundation for his leadership beliefs and actions.

In addition to his duties at Franklin, Dr. Otte serves as a Board Member of State Auto Mutual Insurance Company, an Advisory Board Member for R.C. Olmstead, and has served on several community and educational boards. He holds a bachelor's degree and MBA from Wayne State University, a doctorate in educational leadership from Western Michigan University, and an Honorary Associate Degree from Macomb Community College.

Acknowledgements

This book would not have been possible without the support of the United States Marine Corps. It was Lt. Colonel Pat Messer, USMC (Ret.) who nurtured the idea, and provided invaluable guidance. Major General Terry Murray, Major General Cliff Stanley, and Brigadier General Bill Whitlow (all now retired) provided support in their successive roles as Director of Public Affairs, Headquarters USMC. Also, Sergeant Major Dave Sommers, USMC (Ret.) provided special insights from his service as Sergeant Major of The Marine Corps when General Gray was Commandant. General Carl Mundy and General Chuck Krulak, the 30th and 31st Commandants respectively, not only encouraged the book but provided unique insights. In addition, many other Marines of all ranks contributed in many ways. To all, we are thankful.

In addition, many former Marines took the time to meet and share their experiences in the Corps and relate how they applied what they had learned in the Corps as they became successful in their careers in business, government, and education. Even though we changed from our original intent of including their stories in the book, their messages greatly influenced what we have written and we continue to be grateful to them. They include, in order of their Marine Corps service (along with their organizations at the time of our interviews): Dean Jeffers, General Chairman and CEO, Nationwide Insurance (retired); John Glenn, U.S. Senator (Ohio) and Astronaut; Art Buchwald, Author and Humorist; Bruce Heilman, Chancellor, University of Richmond; Rowland Brown, CEO (retired) of Dorr-Oliver, Buckeye International, and OCLC; Joyce Capps, Federal Judge (retired); Dick Munro, President/CEO, Time Warner (retired); Jim Fisher, Author, President Emeritus CASE; Ben Blaz, U.S. Representative (Guam, retired), Brigadier General, USMC (Ret.); Bud Davis, Chancellor Emeritus, Louisiana State University; Bob Lutz, President and COO, Chrysler Corporation (retired); Major General Richard Alexander, Adjutant General, Ohio National Guard; Hugh McColl, Chairman and CEO, NationsBank; Pat Roberts, U. S. Senator (Kansas); Walter Anderson, Editor PARADE Magazine and Author; Ed Miller, President and CEO, The Equitable Companies Incorporated; Mal Mixon, Chairman and CEO, INVACARE Corporation; Ray Kelly, Undersecretary of the Treasury and (former) NY Police Commissioner; Tom Meeker, President and CEO, Churchill Downs; Jim Kallstrom, (former) Assistant Director, FBI; Jim Webb, Author and (former) Secretary of the Navy; Steve Reinmund, President, Frito-Lay; and Paul McHale, U.S. Congressman (Pennsylvania).

At Franklin University, Jane Robinson, Chief Talent Officer led the efforts of the Franklin University Press. A special thanks to Suzanne Bressoud who served as our diligent editor, and Lori Wengerd who provided valuable insights. Any errors that are left remain the responsibility of the authors.

Personally, we are both indebted to Jan Gray. It was her leadership that kept the project going over a ten-year period. She often provided a gentle hand when it was needed and an even firmer push at the appropriate times.

Finally, an individual acknowledgement, I (Paul Otte) will be forever grateful to General Gray for sending me on a journey that changed my life forever and in the end became a friend. Many times along the way, I felt like pinching myself to see if it all was a dream. Thank you, Sir!

Name Index

P

R

S

T

V

Y

W

Subject Index

D